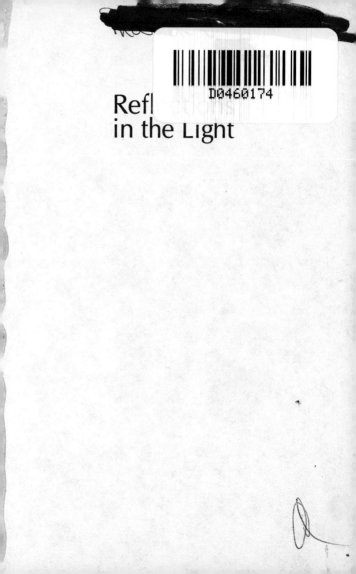

Refl
in the Light

Reflections in the Light

Daily Thoughts and Affirmations

Shakti Gawain

Compiled by
Denise Grimshaw

NEW WORLD LIBRARY • SAN RAFAEL • CALIFORNIA

© 1988 by Shakti Gawain

Based in part on: *Creative Visualization* by Shakti Gawain, © 1978 Shakti Gawain, and *Living in the Light* by Shakti Gawain with Laurel King, © 1986 Shakti Gawain and Laurel King

Published by New World Library
58 Paul Drive, San Rafael, California 94903

Front cover photo and interior photos:
Margaret L. Jackson
Back cover photo: Satyen
Cover design: Kathleen Vande Kieft
Production Coordination: Merrill Peterson
Text design: Abigail Johnston
Typography: Harrington-Young, Albany, California

First printing, September, 1988

Fourth printing, January, 1990

ISBN 0-931432-13-8

ACKNOWLEDGMENTS

I would like to thank Denise Grimshaw for her insight and creativity and for the many hours of research it took to collect all the diverse quotes and compile them into a form that works as a daily meditation over the course of a year.

Special thanks as well to Kathleen Holland for her many helpful suggestions, creative contributions, and hard work editing and organizing the manuscript.

Thanks, too, to Kathryn Altman for coordinating the project, to Marc Allen for his support and encouragement, to Carol LaRusso and Katherine Dieter for their editing and overall help, and to Elizabeth Preim for her assistance in organizing the original manuscript.

The purpose of this book is to give readers an inspirational message, a useful tool, or just some interesting food for thought each day. We hope it will serve to trigger your own thoughts, reactions, and creative ideas.

Almost all of the material in *Reflections In The Light* has been excerpted from my books *Creative Visualization* and *Living In The Light*. In many cases the quotes are verbatim from those books; in most cases they have been edited or revised slightly to stand on their own as daily entries; a few are newly written for this book.

Those of you who have already read my previous books will find this book a handy way to review and remind yourself of familiar concepts and techniques. For those readers who have not read the other books, we have attempted to make each day's entry clear and self-explanatory, but if you have any difficulty understanding the terminology or concepts you may wish to refer to the glossary, or to read the original books in order to gain more clarity.

Each daily entry has a heading, a short message or meditation, and an affirmation. The easiest way to use this book is simply to pick it up and read it at some point each day, and perhaps say the affirmation to yourself a few times throughout the day.

For those who wish to spend a little more time and use this book as a tool for daily study, here is a suggested way to do so. Read the message each morning, think about it (or do the exercise if one is given) and write any responses, feelings, or thoughts that it triggers for you, how it applies to your life, and so on. If you like the affirmation that is given, write it a few times and think of it throughout the day. If you don't care for the affirmation given, write one of your own and use it the same way. In the evening, read it once again and write any further thoughts or experiences you have had in relation to this topic.

There are certain recurring themes throughout the book. In some cases a particular topic may be continued for several days or even a whole month (for example, the month of March is devoted to creative visualization). In other cases, a topic may be introduced for only a day or two and then reappear frequently in later months. In this way, we hope to provide both continuity and variety over the course of a year, no matter what date you begin using the book.

All of us who have worked on this book extend our loving thoughts to you and hope that you find it a useful companion on your journey into the light.

Shakti Gawain

*
**

Winter

**
*

Creating a new way of life

We are living in a very exciting and powerful time. On the deepest level of consciousness, a radical spiritual transformation is taking place. On a worldwide level, we are being challenged to let go of our present way of life and create an entirely new one. We are, in fact, in the process of releasing our old world and building a new world in its place.

The change begins with each individual, but as more and more individuals are being transformed, the mass consciousness is increasingly affected, and the results will be manifested in the world around us.

*

*Each day I am
creating my life
anew.*

*

*As the new emerges,
the old gives way*

For many people this time may be distressing because the world situation and/or our personal lives
may seem to be going from bad to worse. It's as if
many things that used to work are not working
anymore.

Paradoxical as it may seem, these changes are
the most incredible blessing that any of us could
possibly imagine. The simple truth is that the old
way of life has never brought us the deep fulfillment, satisfaction, and joy that we have always
sought. We must let go of the old forms which limit
us or don't fit anymore in order to make way for the
new.

*

*I release
the old and make way
for the new.*

*

Looking within

The old world was based on an external focus. We had come to believe that the material world was the only reality. Thus, feeling essentially lost, empty, and alone, we have continually attempted to find happiness through addiction to external things such as money, material possessions, relationships, work, fame, food or drugs.

Today, as we begin to remember our fundamental spiritual connection, we can look within for the source of our satisfaction, joy, and fulfillment.

*

I find my
spiritual connection
within.

*

Return to kindergarten

Our first task in building the new world is to admit that our "life education" has not necessarily taught us a satisfying way to live. We suffer from a vague sense that there must be something more, some deeper meaning. We must return to kindergarten and start to learn a way of life that is contrary to the way we approached things before—a way of life based on trust of our own inner truth. We can rediscover the child-like innocence and wisdom that knows that anything is possible.

*

I am
learning a new way
of life.

*

The creative power within

The new world is being built as we open to the higher power of the universe and consciously allow that creative energy to move through us. As each of us connects with our spiritual awareness, we learn that the creative power of the universe is within us. We also learn that we can create our own reality and take responsibility for doing so.

*

The creative power
of the universe is now flowing
through me.

*

*Create your life the
way you want it*

Many of us have had the attitude that life is something that happens to us and that all we can do is make the best of it. It is basically a victim's position, giving power to people and things outside of ourselves. We are beginning to realize that the power rests in us, that we can choose to create our life the way we want it to be.

*

*I am now
creating my life
the way I want it
to be.*

*

Light the way

The truth about this earth is that it is an infinitely good, beautiful, and nourishing place to be. The only evil comes from lack of understanding of this truth. Evil (or ignorance) is like a shadow. It is simply a lack of light with no real substance. You cannot cause a shadow to disappear by any form of emotional or physical resistance. In order to cause a shadow to disappear you must shine light on it. By being in touch with the light within, you can dispel the shadow or darkness without struggle.

*

*I am in touch
with the power of my
own light.*

*

Open your eyes to goodness,
beauty, and abundance

Imagine yourself as a successful, satisfied, prosperous, fulfilled person. Really open your eyes to the goodness, beauty, and abundance that are all around you. Imagine this world transformed into a happy, prosperous, and enlightened environment in which everyone can flourish.

*

Today I am
joyful, successful, and
prosperous.

*

Emptiness is filled
from the inside

When we are most unhappy we have a starved feeling in some way. We feel that life in general and other people in particular are not giving us what we need. We try desperately to grasp the love and satisfaction that we crave from outside. Yet we are actually choking off the supply.

The new world is based on trust of the universe within us. We recognize that the creative intelligence and energy of the universe is the fundamental source of everything. Once we connect with this and surrender to it, everything is ours. Emptiness is filled from the inside.

*

I am being
filled from the source
within me.

*

Our guiding force

Once we acknowledge the higher power of the universe, the obvious question arises—"How can we contact this power, or gain access to it?" The knowingness that resides in each of us can be accessed through what we call our intuition. By learning to contact, listen to, and act on our intuition, we can directly connect to the higher power of the universe and allow it to become our guiding force.

*

The higher power
of the universe is
guiding my life through
my intuition.

*

The intuitive mind

The intuitive mind has access to an infinite supply of information. It is able to tap into a deep storehouse of knowledge and wisdom—the universal mind. It is also able to sort out this information and supply us with exactly what we need, when we need it. Our role is to listen to our intuition, trust its guidance, and learn to act on it step by step in our lives.

*

I *trust*
my intuitive
guidance.

*

A *wise being lives*
inside of you

There is a wise being living inside of you. It is your intuitive self. Focus your awareness into a deep place in your body, a place where your "gut feelings" reside. You can communicate with it by silently talking to it, making requests, or asking questions. Then relax, don't think too hard with your mind, and be open to receiving answers. They are usually very simple and relate to the present moment, not the past or future, and they feel right.

*

I trust
the wisdom inside
of me.

*

Step by step, we are
shown the way

Though the messages of the intuitive self may come through a bit at a time, if we learn to follow the supply of information piece by piece, the necessary course of action will unfold. As we learn to rely on this guidance, life takes on a flowing, effortless quality. Our life, feelings, and actions interweave harmoniously with those of others around us.

*

Moment by moment,
I'm learning to trust the flow
of my life.

*

*Trust your feelings and
act on them*

Trust the deepest feelings that you get and act on them. If they are truly from your intuition, you will find that they lead to a feeling of greater aliveness and power and more opportunities begin to open up. If you don't feel more alive and empowered, you may not have been truly acting from your intuition, but from some ego voice in you. The ego seeks what it knows, the familiar, the unchangeable. Often it is based on fear. On the other hand, your intuition never comes from feelings of fear. Go back and ask for clarification and trust your intuition to give you direction.

*

*As I trust
my intuitive feelings and
act on them, I feel
powerful and alive.*

*

Freedom from struggle

We strive so hard to make our lives the way we want them to be. As you begin this day imagine that you can give up struggling for a whole day. Relax for a while, and trust that your needs will be met by the natural flow of life.

The philosophy of *being here now* and letting go of attachment is a very freeing experience. When you do this, you discover that you're really perfectly okay, in fact you feel quite wonderful. You can just let yourself be, let the world be, and give up the struggle of trying to change things.

*

*I relax
and let myself
be.*

*

Change

Change happens not by trying to *make* yourself change, but by being conscious of what's *not* working. You can then ask your higher self for help in releasing the old and bringing in the new pattern. Remember, the darkest hour is just before the dawn—change often occurs just when you've given up, or when you least expect it.

*

*I am
open and willing
to change.*

*

Follow your creative energy

To whatever degree you listen to and follow your intuition, you will become a creative channel for the higher power of the universe to the same degree. When you willingly follow where your creative energy leads, the higher power can come through you to manifest its creative work. When this happens you will find yourself flowing with energy, transforming everything around you.

*

As I follow
my intuition, creative energy
flows through me.

*

You are a channel
for creativity

We have a common power source (the universe) and the same creative energy flows through each of us. To be a channel is to be in touch with and bring forth the wisdom and creativity of your own deepest source. To be a channel is to be fully and freely yourself, consciously aware that you are an expression of the highest creativity of the universe.

*

I am a
channel for the creative power
of the universe.

*

Higher purpose

We each have a significant contribution to make in this lifetime. I call this contribution our higher purpose. It always involves being yourself totally, completely and naturally, and doing something or many things that you genuinely love to do, that come easily to you. As you learn to follow your feelings, dreams and visions, to explore doing things you love, you begin to discover your higher purpose.

Every moment is a moment of creation and each moment of creation contains infinite possibilities.

*

*By being myself and
doing what I love, I make
a significant contribution
to life.*

*

Fulfillment is found
in daily life

Fulfillment comes from what you are doing at this very moment. It is not a matter of doing things now for gratification later. (I will work now so I can get a better job later. I will work hard now, so that I can retire and enjoy life. I will work hard now to have enough money for a vacation.) It is the fulfillment of what you are doing now that counts. Even the simplest things are significant.

*

I find
fulfillment in everything
I do.

*

Being, doing, and having

We can think of life having three dimensions: being, doing, and having. Often we attempt to live our lives backwards. We try to *have* more money in order to feel we can *do* more of what we want, so we can *be* happier. The way it actually works is the reverse. We must first *be* who we really are, then *do* what we feel guided to do, in order to *have* what we want.

*

*I allow myself
to be; I do what feels right;
I have everything
I truly want.*

*

Letting go

Let us imagine that life is a river. Most people are clinging to the bank, afraid to let go and risk being carried along by the current of the river. When the pain of hanging on becomes greater than the fear of letting go, we let go and the river begins to carry us along safely. Once we are used to being in the flow of the river, we can begin to look ahead and guide our course. We choose which of the many branches of the river we prefer to follow, all the while still going with the flow. We can enjoy being here now, flowing with *what is* and at the same time, guide ourselves consciously toward our goals by taking full responsibility for creating our own lives.

*

*As I relax
and let go, I flow toward
my greatest good.*

*

Living in harmony with the universe

Although letting go of the old world may seem difficult at times, it is well worth whatever it takes to make the transition into the new world. We are now learning to live in accordance with the true laws of the universe. Living in harmony with the universe is living full of joy, power, love, and abundance.

*

*I am
living in harmony with
the universe.*

*

Spirit and form

Spirit is the essence of consciousness, the energy of the universe that creates all things. Each one of us is a part of that spirit—a divine entity. So the spirit is the higher self, the eternal being that lives within us.

Form is the physical world: body, mind, personality. We as spiritual beings created the physical world as a place to learn. We're here to learn how to master the process of creation—to learn how to consciously channel the creative energy of spirit into physical form.

*

*I am
learning to create form
from spirit.*

*

What is creative visualization?

Creative visualization is the technique of using your imagination to create what you want in your life. You are already using it every day, every minute in fact. It is your natural power of imagination, the basic creative energy of the universe which you use constantly whether or not you are aware of it. All you have to do is relax deeply and picture a desired goal in your mind exactly the way you want it to be.

*

*I am now
visualizing my life exactly the
way I want it.*

*

Contacting the source

One of the most important steps in making creative
visualization work is to have the experience of
connecting with your inner creative source. I like to
think of contacting the source as connecting with
your higher self, the god-like being who dwells
within you. Being in contact with your higher self is
characterized by a deep sense of knowingness. You
know that you are creating your own world and that
you have infinite power to create it as you desire.

*

*I am in contact
with my source and
am creating my life as I
desire it to be.*

*

Our divine potential

There is no separation between God and us. We are divine expressions of the creative principle on this level of existence. We contain the potential for everything within us. Manifestation through creative visualization is the process of realizing and making visible on the physical plane our divine potential.

*

I *am*
a divine expression
of God.

*

Have fun with it

Get comfortable. Relax your body. Breathe deeply and slowly. Start to imagine something you want, exactly as you would like it. Have fun with it. Pretend you are a child daydreaming about what you want for your birthday. Now, keeping the idea or image still in your mind, mentally make some very positive, affirmative statements to yourself. End your visualization with a firm statement to yourself. "This or something better now manifests for me in totally satisfying and harmonious ways for the highest good of all concerned."

*

I *have*
fun visualizing what
I *want.*

*

A *source deep within*

As we explore the process of creating our own reality, we begin to realize that the creative power we are feeling is coming from some source other than our personality/ego selves. It seems to come from some place deep within ourselves. We become interested in discovering what this creative force is and how it works. We realize that "it" (our higher self) knows more than "I" (our personality self). We find out what the inner guidance is telling us and follow it.

*

*I feel
creative power coming from
deep within me.*

*

Your own personal sanctuary

Close your eyes, relax your body, imagine yourself in a beautiful, natural environment—somewhere where you feel comfortable, relaxed, and peaceful. Explore your environment, noticing details, sounds, and smells. Do anything you would like to make the place more home-like and comfortable. Build a house or shelter or just surround the whole area with a golden light of protection and safety. From now on this is your own personal inner sanctuary. You will always find it healing and relaxing. It is a place of special power.

*

Within me
is a special place of serenity
and power.

*

Enlightenment

When we begin to open up to a spiritual path, we may go through many different experiences and processes in our search, but eventually we come back to an experience of our true selves, the godlike nature or universal mind that is within us all. Through this experience we are eventually restored to our full spiritual power. The emptiness inside us is filled up from within. This is the process known as enlightenment.

*

I am being
filled with my full
spiritual power.

*

*There is a higher
intelligence*

The foundation for life in the new world we are
creating is built on the understanding that there is a
higher intelligence, a fundamental creative power
or energy in the universe which is the substance of
all that exists.

Many terms are used to express an experience of
this power. Although it is difficult to convey with
words and rational concepts, each of us has at some
time felt a sense of oneness, knowingness, and
unity with the divine presence.

*

*I feel
the presence of a power
greater than myself.*

*

A presence within us

As we surrender to the power of the universe and trust it more, we find our relationship with this higher essence becoming more personal. We can literally feel a presence within us, guiding us, loving us, teaching us, encouraging us. The universe can be teacher, guide, friend, mother, father, lover, creative genius, fairy godmother, even Santa Claus. In other words, whatever we feel we need or want can be fulfilled through this inner connection.

*

I have a personal
relationship with a
higher power.

*

Distinguishing intuition

Your intuition is always one hundred percent correct, but it takes time to hear it correctly. If you are willing to risk acting on what you believe to be true and risk making mistakes, you will learn very fast by paying attention to what works and what doesn't work. The first step is to pay more attention to what you feel inside, to the dialogue that goes on within you. Through practice you will be able to distinguish your intuitive voice from other thoughts and voices.

*

*I am hearing
my intuition more clearly
every day.*

*

Observe your inner dialogue

Anyone who has practiced meditation knows how difficult it can be to quiet our "mind talk" in order to connect with our deeper, wise, intuitive mind. One traditional meditation practice is to simply observe the inner dialogue as objectively as possible. This is a valuable experience that allows you to become aware of the types of thoughts you habitually think. Many of these thoughts come from programming we picked up long ago, which is still influencing us. Once we recognize these thought patterns we can begin to change old habits. We can tell the difference between the limiting, habitual mind talk, and the voice of our inner guidance.

*

*I pay
attention to the thoughts
I think.*

*

A natural human experience

When we speak of following your inner voice, remember that most people do not experience it as a voice. Often it's more like a feeling, an energy, a sense of "I want to do this," or "I don't want to do this." It's a simple, natural, human experience that we have lost touch with and need to reclaim.

*

*I reclaim
my natural ability to trust
my intuition.*

*

Contacting intuition

Get in a comfortable position, sitting or lying down.
Close your eyes and relax. Take several deep, slow,
long breaths and as you exhale each time, imagine
relaxing your body and relaxing your mind. Then
imagine moving your awareness into a very deep
place inside of you—deep in your solar plexus or
your belly. Keep going deeper until you find a quiet
resting place inside. Imagine that in that deep place
you contact your own inner truth. Ask if there is a
message for you or something you need to know or
remember. Or ask a specific question. Then relax
and feel or "listen" to what comes to you. It may be
a thought, a feeling, or an image. Just receive whatever comes. Don't try to figure it out with your mind
or you will block the process. If it seems like nothing
happens, don't worry about it. Practice this regularly in a relaxed way, and you will begin to feel
more in touch with your intuition.

*

I am
in touch with my intuitive
feelings.

*

Practice listening

It takes practice to hear and trust your intuition. The more you do it, the easier it will become. Eventually you will be in touch with your intuitive feelings much of the time. Ask yourself questions. Know that the wise being within you, an incredible source of power and strength, is available to answer your questions and guide you. As you grow more sensitive to this guidance from the intuitive feelings from within, you will gain a sense of knowing what you need to do in any situation.

*

*I trust
my inner knowing in
all situations.*

*

Just be yourself

It isn't necessary to be perfect to be a channel for the universe. You just have to be real. Be yourself. The more honest and spontaneous you are, the more freely the creative force can flow through you. As it does, it cleans out the remnants of old blockages. The more you are true to yourself, the clearer your channel gets.

*

*Today I am
honest, spontaneous, and
true to myself.*

*

We are all geniuses

We are all geniuses, each in our own unique way. We discover the nature of our particular genius when we stop trying to conform to our own or other people's models, and learn to be ourselves, allowing our natural channel to open. Then we discover that we each have something special to offer to the world that no one else can duplicate.

*

*In my
own unique way, I am
a genius.*

*

Every creative genius
has been a channel

Every creative genius has been a channel for the divine power of the universe. Every master work has been created through the channeling process. Great works are not created by the ego alone. They *arise* from a deep inspiration on the universal level, and are then expressed and brought into form *through* the individual ego and personality.

*

I am
a channel for creative
inspiration.

*

We each have unique gifts

In creating our new world, things may come together in unexpected ways and fascinating combinations. Perhaps you haven't found your career because it doesn't exist yet. Your particular and unique way of expressing yourself has never existed before and will never be repeated again.

*

*I am
discovering my own
unique expression.*

*

Experiencing our feelings

When we have suppressed and closed off our feelings, we cannot contact the universe within us. We cannot hear our intuitive voice, and we certainly can't enjoy being alive. When we are willing to fully experience a particular feeling such as fear, anger, loneliness, or confusion and embrace that emotion without judgment, the blocked energy releases quickly and the feeling dissolves, allowing us to feel more peaceful and open.

*

*I accept
and experience all
my feelings.*

*

Rainbow colors of life

There are no such things as negative or positive feelings. We make them negative or positive by our rejection or acceptance of them. All feelings are part of the wonderful, ever-changing sensation of being alive. If we love all the different feelings, they become so many rainbow colors of life.

*

*All my feelings
are a natural expression
of life.*

*

Falling in love
with ourselves

When we fall in love with someone, we are also falling in love with aspects of ourselves that we see reflected in that person. We may feel that our loved one has qualities that we don't have, but those qualities exist in us too and are as yet undiscovered or undeveloped.

Today, think of each person you love and imagine him or her as a mirror, reflecting your own beauty and lovability. The more you can love yourself through these reflections, the more you can truly love and appreciate others.

*

I am
falling in love
with myself.

*

We can have everything

As long as we focus only on the outer world there will always be an empty, hungry, lost place inside us that needs to be filled. When we keep our focus on the universe inside, we can have everything external—money, success, and fulfilling relationships, as well as that incredible connection inside ourselves.

*

I *am receiving*
everything from the
source within me.

*

Feeling more alive

Each time that we choose to trust and follow our intuition our channel opens more. More of the life force flows through. The cells of our body actually receive more energy, renewing and revitalizing faster. Physically, emotionally, and mentally we feel more alive. More of our spirit light can shine through. Our body stays young, healthy, beautiful, and radiates vitality.

*

I feel
the life force flowing
through my body.

*

Surrender to life

A part of us wants life, wants to make the commitment to live, and is willing to trust our intuition and follow it from moment to moment. There is also a part of us that doesn't trust this inclination. "I can't do this, it's too much, too intense. I don't want to surrender." When we distrust this inclination we experience only effort and struggle. When we surrender to life the flow of energy increases, and we feel the passion of being alive.

*

I
surrender
to life.

*

The moment of total
surrender

When we finally give up the struggle to find fulfillment outside of ourselves, we have nowhere to go but within. It is at this moment of total surrender that the light begins to dawn. We expect to hit bottom, but instead we fall through a trap door into a bright new world. We have rediscovered the world of our spirit.

*

Through
surrender, I find the light
within me.

*

Asking for guidance

If you have a problem that you need help with, try this technique. Sit or lie down in a comfortable position, close your eyes, take a few deep breaths and relax deeply. Imagine that you are in touch with your deepest inner wisdom. Formulate the problem in your mind, and ask for guidance from that inner source. Relax for a few minutes and be receptive to any feelings, images, or thoughts that come to you. The guidance may come to you right away, or it may come sometime within the next few hours or days.

*

I am
asking for and listening to
my inner guidance.

*

Take a moment

One important step in learning to hear and follow
your intuition is to simply practice checking in
regularly, at least twice a day, more often if possible.
Take a moment or two to relax and listen to your gut
feelings. Cultivate this habit of communicating with
your inner self. Ask for help and guidance when you
need it and practice listening for answers.

*

I

*listen to my gut
feelings.*

*

It takes practice

We need to re-educate ourselves to listen to and trust the inner truths that come to us through our intuitive feelings. We must learn to act on them, even though it may feel risky and frightening at first, because we are no longer playing it safe, doing what we "should" do, pleasing others, following rules, or deferring to outside authority.

Learning to trust our intuition is an art form, and like all other art forms, it takes practice to perfect. We have to be willing to make "mistakes," to try something and fail, and then try something different the next time. If we hold back out of fear of being wrong, learning to trust our intuition could take a lifetime.

*

I am
learning to trust
my intuition.

*

Don't push yourself

You can't always force yourself to follow your intuitive feelings. Sometimes it simply feels too difficult or scary. Don't push past what you are ready to do. Simply observe the process and be honest with yourself about how it feels and what happens. If you love and accept yourself exactly as you are, change will happen naturally and spontaneously.

*

Today
I love myself and
accept myself exactly as
I am.

*

*Each of us plays a
unique instrument*

We each play a unique instrument in the orchestra
of life. If we play our part without regard for the
conductor's direction or the rest of the orchestra,
then we have total chaos. If we try to take our cues
only from those around us, it will be impossible to
achieve harmony. However, if we watch the conductor (our intuition) and follow its direction, we can
experience the joy of playing our unique part, and at
the same time experience ourselves as part of a
greater harmonious whole.

*

*I am
a unique and special
instrument.*

*

We receive the support
we need

If we are honest with ourselves, we will readily admit that we are not making great music on the guidance of our rational mind alone. By tuning into our intuition and allowing it to become the guiding force in our lives, we allow the conductor to take his rightful place as leader of the orchestra. Rather than losing our individual freedom, we receive the support we need to express our individuality.

*

In harmony
with the whole, I find my
individual freedom.

*

See yourself as a channel

As you start this day, spend a few minutes seeing yourself as a channel for the universe. Feel the energy in your body and be aware of your ability to channel the light to others. With each person you meet and each exchange you have, realize the light of the universe is moving through you to them.

*

I am
channeling the light to
each person I meet.

*

Everyone is a channel
for the universe

As you focus on the channel in each person you're with, you will see that every exchange you have with them is the universe talking to you. As you acknowledge your own true power and that of others, the light will grow. You will begin to see the light and the gift in every situation.

Feel and acknowledge this for the entire day today, with everyone you meet.

*

Today I see
the gift I receive from
every person I meet.

*

Never alone

When you begin to see yourself as a channel, you will seldom feel truly alone anymore. In fact, it is in physical aloneness that you will often find the most powerful communion with the higher power. At such times, the previously empty places inside of you are filled with light. Here you will find a constant guiding presence that tells you which move to make next, and helps you to learn the lesson that lies in taking each step along your path.

*

*I love
being alone with the
higher power.*

*

Becoming a channel for the universe

To become a clear channel for the universe presents the highest challenge and offers the greatest potential joy and fulfillment for every human being. Being a channel means living fully and passionately in the world, having deep relationships, playing, working, creating, enjoying money and material possessions, being yourself, yet never for one moment losing your profound connection with the power of the universe within you.

*

I *am living fully*
and passionately as a clear
channel.

*

You are like a
golden sun

Sit or lie in a comfortable position. Let your body relax completely. Breathe deeply and slowly. Visualize a light within your heart—glowing, radiant and warm. Feel it spreading and growing, shining out from you further and further until you are like a golden sun radiating loving energy on everything and everyone around you. Say to yourself, "Divine light and divine love are flowing through me and radiating from me to everything around me." Repeat this over and over until you have a strong sense of your own spiritual energy.

*

Divine light and
divine love are flowing
through me.

*

Creative visualization is magic

Creative visualization is magic in the truest and highest meaning of the word. It involves understanding and aligning yourself with the natural principles that govern the workings of the universe and learning to use these principles in the most conscious and creative way.

*

*I feel the magic
of the universe operating
in my life.*

*

"As you sow, so shall you reap"

Consciously having an idea or thought, and holding it in your mind is a process which will tend to attract and create that form on the material plane. "As you sow, so shall you reap." What this means is that we always attract into our lives whatever we think about most, believe in most strongly, expect on the deepest level, and imagine most vividly.

*

Today I am
attracting beauty, joy, and
abundance into my life.

*

Use creative visualization
consciously

In the past, many of us have used our power of creative visualization in a relatively unconscious way. Because of our own deep-seated negative concepts about life, we have automatically and unconsciously expected and imagined lack, limitation, difficulties, and problems to be our lot in life. To one degree or another, we have created these difficulties for ourselves.

Now we have the opportunity to use the conscious power of our minds to create self-love, abundance, freedom, and joy in our lives.

*

Today
I expect the
best.

*

Everything is energy

Everything in the physical world is made of energy, all vibrating at different rates of speed. Thought is a relatively fine, light form of energy and is quick and easy to change. Matter is relatively dense and com- pact energy, slower to move and change. All these energy fields are interconnected, so how we think and feel is constantly affecting and being affected by everything around us. We are all part of one great energy flow.

*

I *feel*
at one with the energy
of the universe.

*

We create first in
thought form

When we create something we always create it first in thought form. An artist first has an idea or inspiration, then creates a painting. The idea is like a blueprint. It creates an image of the form which then magnetizes and guides the physical energy to flow into that form and eventually manifests on the physical plane.

*

My thoughts are
creating a wonderful blueprint
for my life.

*

*Imagination is the ability
to create*

The use of creative visualization gives us a key to tap into the natural goodness and bounty of life. Imagination is the ability to create an idea or mental picture in your mind. In creative visualization you use your imagination to create a clear image, sense, or feeling of something you wish to manifest.

*

*My imagination
is a powerful tool for
creation.*

*

Relax deeply

It is important to relax deeply when we are first learning to use creative visualization. When our minds and bodies are deeply relaxed and centered, our brainwaves change and become slower. As we are able to silence our habitual mind chatter, we have a chance to listen on a deeper level. We become receptive and open to our creative imagination and intuition.

*

I *am*
deeply relaxed and
centered.

*

A basic creative visualization
exercise

Think of something you desire to have, to do, or to experience. For this exercise, pick something simple and fairly realistic for you.

Sit or lie down in a comfortable position. Take a few long, slow, deep breaths and relax your body and mind. Now imagine yourself doing, having, or experiencing whatever it is that you want. Imagine it as if it is already happening, as if it is true, now. You might see a mental picture of it, or just get a feeling or a sense of what it would be like for you if this wish came true. Let yourself enjoy the experience.

When you feel complete, open your eyes. Know that in visualizing or imagining your goal as if it were already true, you have opened the door to creating it. Repeat this exercise whenever you want to.

*

This or
something better is now
coming true.

*

Visualizing your goal

Bring your idea or mental picture to mind often, both in quiet meditation periods and also casually throughout the day when you happen to think about it. This way it becomes an integrated part of your life. It becomes more a reality for you and you project it more successfully. Focus on it clearly, yet in a light, gentle way. It is important not to feel like you're working too hard for it, or putting excessive amounts of energy into it. That would hinder rather than help.

*

*I focus on
my goals in a gentle,
relaxed way.*

*

To affirm means to make firm

An affirmation is a strong, positive statement that something is already so. It is a way of making firm that which you are imagining. While you are using affirmations, try to temporarily suspend any doubts or disbelief you may have, at least for the moment. Practice getting the feeling that that which you desire is very real and possible.

*

*What
I desire is
possible.*

*

Finding the right affirmation

Always choose affirmations that feel totally right for you. What works for one person may not work at all for another. An affirmation should feel positive, expansive, freeing, and/or supportive. If it doesn't, find another one or try changing the words until it feels right. A powerful, effective affirmation may bring up some resistance from the part of you that fears change, but that will dissolve as you work with it. Choose affirmations that feel supportive, freeing, and expansive.

*

I am now discovering
the most powerful affirmations
for me.

*

Affirmations from the heart

In general, the shorter and simpler the affirmation, the more effective. An affirmation should be a clear statement that conveys a strong feeling. The more feeling it conveys, the stronger impression it makes on your mind. Affirmations that are long, wordy, and theoretical lose their emotional impact. Choose affirmations that come from your heart, not your head.

*

*As I listen to
my heart, the right affirmation
comes to me.*

*

Resistance to change

You may feel emotional resistance to any affirmation when you first use it, especially one which is really powerful for you and is going to make a real change in your consciousness. That is simply our initial resistance to change and growth. If doubts or contradicting thoughts arise, don't resist them or try to prevent them. This will tend to give them a power they don't otherwise have. Just let your doubts flow through your consciousness and then return to your positive statements and images.

*

*I accept
my resistance and move
forward.*

*

A *daily endeavor*

If possible, use creative visualization and affirmations a little each day, even if only for five minutes. It is especially good to do creative visualization at night just before sleeping or in the morning just after awakening, because at those times the mind and body often are already deeply relaxed and receptive. A short period of meditation and creative visualization done at midday will relax and renew you and will cause your day to flow more smoothly.

*

I am now
using creative visualization
every day.

*

Creative visualization—receptive
and active

There are two aspects to creative visualization—receptive and active. In the receptive mode we ask questions and receive answers or guidance from our intuitive mind through words, mental images, or feelings. In the active mode we choose mental images and affirmations and use them as tools to consciously create our reality. Both aspects are important parts of the creative process.

*

I am developing
the receptive and active aspects
of my imagination.

*

Goals give us direction

Every time you have a desire, in a certain sense you have a goal, something you would like to be, do, or have. Some desires are merely passing fancies, but others stay with us and go deeper. Our desires and our goals give us direction and focus. They help point us down our path of action in life.

*

My desires and goals
give me positive direction
in life.

*

Creating on many levels

Your goal may be on any level—physical, emotional, mental, or spiritual. You might imagine yourself with a new home or a new job, or having a beautiful relationship, or feeling calm and serene. You might picture yourself handling a difficult situation effortlessly or simply see yourself as a radiant being filled with light and love. You can work on any level and all will have results.

*

I am creating
positive results on all levels
of my life.

*

Enjoy the entire journey

To enjoy your goals, think of them as signposts, pointing you in a certain direction. They give you a focus and help your energy to get moving. The way you go is up to you; you can get very uptight focusing only on getting to your goal or you can relax and enjoy the entire journey, appreciating every unexpected bend and turn of the road, every new opportunity for learning and feeling.

*

I am relaxing
and enjoying every moment of
my journey.

*

Dissolving barriers

Creative visualization is a means of unblocking or dissolving the barriers we ourselves have created to the naturally harmonious, abundant, and loving flow of the universe. It is only truly effective when it is used in alignment with our highest goals and purposes for the highest good of all beings.

*

*I am dissolving
my barriers and finding
my highest good.*

*

*Having what we want
supports others*

Because human nature is basically loving, most of us will not allow ourselves to have what we want so long as we believe that we might be depriving others in order to do so. We have to understand in a deep way that living a fulfilling life contributes to the general state of human happiness and inspires and supports others to create more happiness for themselves.

*

*The more
I receive, the more others are
able to receive.*

*

See yourself receiving

As you focus on your goal, make strong positive affirmations to yourself that it has come, or is now coming to you. See yourself receiving or achieving it. Always phrase affirmations in the present tense, not in the future. Don't say "I will get a wonderful new job," but rather "I now have a wonderful new job." This is not lying to yourself, but is acknowledging the fact that everything is created first on the mental plane before it can manifest in objective reality. It is also a way of changing the patterns of how we usually talk to ourselves.

*

*I am
achieving my goals
easily.*

*

Every moment is an opportunity

Remember that you are always creating your life new and fresh. You are not trying to redo or change what already exists. To do so would be to resist what is, which creates struggle and conflict. Take the attitude that you are accepting and handling whatever exists in your life and at the same time recognizing that every moment is a new opportunity to begin creating exactly what you desire and will make you the happiest.

*

I
*create my life anew
each day.*

*

Desire, belief, and acceptance

Creative visualization will work successfully for you if you have the desire for, belief in, and acceptance of your goal. You must have a strong and true *desire* to have or create that which you have chosen. The more you *believe* in your chosen goal, the more able you will be to create it. And you must be willing to *accept* and have that which you are seeking. Together these three elements form a clear intention to manifest your dream.

*

I *desire,*
believe in, and accept my
highest good.

*

With perseverance you will succeed

Don't feel discouraged if you don't immediately feel totally successful with your creative visualization. Remember that most of us have had years of negative thought patterns to overcome, so be patient. It has taken a lifetime to create your world the way it is. It may not necessarily change instantly, although it often does. With perseverance you will succeed in creating what seem like many miracles in your life.

*

In my own time and
my own way, I am creating
miracles in my life.

*

Flow with the moment

Continue to work on the process of affirmations and visualizations until you achieve your goal, or no longer have the desire to do so. If you lose interest it may mean that it is time for a new look at what you want. If you find that a goal has changed for you, be sure to acknowledge that to yourself. This helps you avoid getting confused or feeling like you've failed, when you have simply changed. Be willing to flow with the moment. It is easier to be clear about your desire, if you are willing to change as your life changes around you.

*

*As the
flow of life changes,
I change.*

*

The highest good for all

Creative visualization cannot be used to control the behavior of others or cause them to do something against their will. Its effect is to dissolve our internal barriers to natural harmony and self-realization, allowing everybody to manifest in their most positive way.

*

As I manifest
my own highest good,
I allow others to
manifest theirs.

*

Writing your goals

Write your most important goals for the next month, six months, year and/or five years. Write each one in the form of an affirmation; that is, write it in a sentence, in the present tense, as if it had already come true. So, instead of saying "I want to live in a bigger, sunnier, more beautiful apartment," phrase it this way—"I am now living in a big, beautiful, sunny apartment that I love." This will make it a powerful process of creative visualization.

*

*I am achieving
my goals easily, effortlessly,
and harmoniously.*

*

Do something wonderful for yourself

When you achieve a goal, be sure to acknowledge consciously to yourself that it has been completed. Often we achieve things which we have been desiring and visualizing, and we forget to even notice that we have succeeded. So give yourself some appreciation, not just a pat on the back. Do something wonderful for yourself and be sure to thank the universe for fulfilling your request.

*

*I love and
appreciate myself and the
universe within me.*

*

In the spirit of the Tao

The only effective way to use creative visualization is in the spirit of the Tao—going with the flow. That means that you don't have to struggle to get where you want to go. You simply put out clearly to the universe where you would like to go, and then patiently and harmoniously follow the flow of the river of life until it takes you there or somewhere even better.

*

I patiently
trust in the power of
the universe.

*

Pink bubble

Relax, sit, or lie down comfortably, close your eyes and breathe deeply. Imagine something you would like to manifest. Imagine that it has already happened. Picture it, sense it, feel it. Now, surround your fantasy with a pink bubble. Put your goal inside the bubble. Pink is the color associated with the heart, and if this color vibration surrounds whatever you visualize, it will bring to you only that which is in perfect affinity with your being. Now, let go of the bubble and imagine it floating off into the hands of the universe. Release it, knowing the universe will bring this (or something better) to you at the right time.

*

*My heart's
desire is coming
true.*

*

*You are the constant creator
of your life*

As you develop the habit of using creative visualization and begin to trust the results it can bring to you, you will find it becomes a state of consciousness in which you know that you are the constant creator of your life. That is the ultimate point of creative visualization: to make every moment of our lives a moment of wondrous creation in which we are just naturally choosing the best, the most beautiful, the most fulfilling lives we can imagine.

*

*My life
is my wondrous
creation.*

*

**

Spring

**

The fool

The archetype of the fool can connect us with a very important aspect of ourselves. It is the image of the innocent, childlike person who is not caught in the concepts and stereotypes of the rational, sophisticated mind and therefore is free to perceive and experience life directly as it really is, in the moment.

For today, let go of your adult sophistication and allow yourself to experience the simple delight of a very young child. Be the fool, who, having no complex concepts of how things *should* be, simply enjoys life as it is.

*

I am
filled with innocent
delight.

*

Our female aspect

The female aspect of our being is our intuitive self. This is the deepest, wisest part of ourselves and is the feminine energy in both men and women. It is the receptive aspect, the open door through which the higher intelligence of the universe can flow, the receiving end of the channel. Our female self communicates to us through our intuition. Those inner promptings, gut feelings, or images come from a deep place within us.

*

*I listen to
and honor my inner
female.*

*

Our male aspect

The male aspect of ourselves is action. It is our ability to do things in the physical world—to think, to speak, to move our bodies. Whether you are a man or a woman, your masculine energy enables you to act. It is the outflowing end of the channel. The feminine receives the universal creative energy and the masculine expresses it in the world through action. Thus we have the creative process.

*

*I honor
and express my inner
male.*

*

Following our natural rhythm

There is a natural rhythm to the active and receptive energies within us. At times our energy is strong and outgoing—it is time to pursue our goals, take risks, get things accomplished. At other times, our energy is quiet and sensitive, and we need to take time to nurture ourselves, relax, and just "be" for awhile. As we trust and follow this rhythm, we attract everything we need and create everything we truly desire.

*

I am
following the natural rhythm
of my energy.

*

*Channeling money is a
creative process*

There are active and receptive aspects to the process of channeling money as in every other creative process. The masculine or active way of making money is to go out after something. You see something you want and go for it. The feminine or receptive way of making money is to attract that which you want to you. We need to develop both active and receptive aspects so that money can flow freely in our lives.

*

*Money is flowing
freely and abundantly into
my life.*

*

Heal your feelings

In the process of learning to trust your intuition, many old feelings and deep emotional patterns will come to the surface to be healed and released. Feelings of sadness, fear, pain, guilt, and rage may come up. Allow yourself to consciously experience and accept these feelings; as you do so they will naturally begin to release and heal. As the light of awareness penetrates every cell of your body, it dispels the darkness.

*

As I allow
myself to feel my feelings,
I heal them.

*

Replacing the outer shell

Many of us have been taught to be very intellectual,
very active, and to drive ourselves very hard. We may
have a strongly developed intuition, but have not
put it in charge. In fact, we may ignore it a lot of the
time. We basically protect our sensitive, vulnerable
feelings by erecting a tough outer shell. As we begin
to use our inner strength and power to take care of
ourselves, honor our need for relaxation, and protect our tender feelings, the outer shell melts away
and leaves us open yet strong.

*

*I am
strong and
open.*

*

Allow your feelings to flow

Acceptance of our feelings is directly related to becoming a creative channel. If you don't allow your feelings to flow, your channel will be blocked. If you've stored up a lot of unfelt or unexpressed emotions, you have a lot of hurt, frightened, angry voices inside which make it difficult to hear the more subtle voice of your intuition. Find a safe place, alone or with a therapist or support group, and allow yourself to express the feelings within you through words, sounds, and/or movement.

*

*I allow
my feelings to be expressed
and released.*

*

Change can feel uncomfortable

In being true to yourself you will feel more alive; you also may feel uncomfortable. This is because you are risking change. You may experience intense emotions. Allow these emotions their full expression. After all, your inner guidance may have to move through years of accumulated unconscious doubt and fear. Simply let the feelings come up and flush through you. They are being cleaned out and healed by the light of your spirit.

*

*I accept all
the feelings that come with
change and growth.*

*

Feel more joy

Sadness is related to the opening of your heart. If you allow yourself to feel sad, especially if you can cry, you will find that your heart opens wider and you can feel more love and more joy.

*

*As I allow myself
to feel my sadness, I open
to more joy.*

*

Listen to all your feelings

If there seems to be an unhappy or upset feeling inside of you, give it a voice and listen to that feeling. Ask it to talk to you and tell you what it's feeling. Try to hear it and listen to its point of view. Be sympathetic, loving, and supportive towards your feelings. Ask if there is anything you could do to take better care of yourself.

*

I love
and support all my feelings
today.

*

Experience ecstasy

Some of our spiritual models reflect our good ideas more than they reveal an actual picture of enlightenment. Many people want to be mellow, positive, and loving all the time, which really is an expression of the ego's need to feel in control, instead of allowing and trusting our true feelings to show. As the ego releases its need to control, and we trust ourselves more and more to allow the full range of our feelings to emerge, we naturally experience the ecstasy of life.

*

*It's safe
for me to release control
and experience the ecstasy
of life.*

*

Be good to yourself

If I'm feeling sad, I might crawl into bed and cry, taking time to be very loving and nurturing to myself. Or I might find someone caring to talk to who will simply listen to me until some of the feelings are released and I feel lighter. If I've been working too hard, I learn to put work aside no matter how important it seems. I take time to play, or take a hot bath, or read a novel. If someone I love wants something from me that I don't want to give, I learn to say no, firmly, yet with love. I trust that he or she will be better off than if I did it when I didn't want to. This way when I say "yes" I really mean it.

*

*I take
good care of
myself.*

*

Renewing our bodies

When we aren't following the flow of energy, life becomes a struggle. Stress and strain take their toll on the physical form. Lines of worry form and the body begins to bend with the effort it is making. If we continue to choose to close off the energy— moment after moment, day after day, year after year—eventually the body will age, deteriorate and die. When we change our pattern and begin to trust ourselves more, the body begins to renew itself and becomes healthy and filled with life energy.

*

As I *follow*
the flow of life, my body grows
healthy and vital.

*

From mind to body

Creative visualization is a way in which we communicate from our minds to our bodies. It is the process of forming images and thoughts of our desires consciously or unconsciously and then sending them to our bodies as clear messages. Our bodies respond by manifesting those thoughts and images into physical form. The more loving and positive the messages we send, the healthier, stronger and more vital our bodies become.

*

I am sending clear,
loving thought messages from
my mind to my body.

*

Love your body

Show your body how much you appreciate and respect it. Your body has been criticized, judged, and rejected by you for years. It will respond quickly to love and energy. You will feel lighter and more energized. You will start looking more beautiful. Lines in your face will relax. You will glow with strength and health. You will be amazed at the results of loving your body.

*

*I appreciate,
love, and respect my
body.*

*

Express the beauty of your spirit

As you find new ways to appreciate your body, you will see it change and become lighter, stronger, more clearly defined, and more beautiful. You will have a sense of the light shining through you. Because your life is your creation and the mirror of your transformation, all forms in your life will increasingly express the power and beauty of your spirit.

*

*My body
is a beautiful expression
of my spirit.*

*

Accept the best

Many of us have difficulty accepting the best. This usually stems from some basic feelings of unworthiness which we took on at a very early age. If you find that you have difficulty imagining yourself in the most wonderful possible circumstances, it might be time to take a good look at your self-image. By accepting and loving yourself, you will be willing and able to accept the best that life has to offer you.

*

*I deserve
the very best in
my life.*

*

Self-image

To get in touch with your self-image, begin to ask yourself "How do I feel about myself right now?" at various times throughout the day. Just begin to notice what kinds of ideas or images you hold in mind about yourself at different times. Observe whether you frequently tell yourself negative or critical things about yourself. Once you understand the ways in which you are not loving yourself, begin to regularly tell yourself positive, appreciative, loving things. Think of specific qualities that you do appreciate about yourself.

*

*I love
and appreciate myself
as I am now.*

*

Self-esteem list

Imagine you are your own best friend. Describe yourself exactly as your friend would if he or she was telling someone else about you. Use your own name and tell about all of your good qualities and characteristics. "I can always depend on John when I need help," or "John has a delightful sense of humor and always helps me to laugh when I am taking myself too seriously."

As you do this exercise, either have someone else take notes or write down what you are describing about yourself. Now you have the beginning of your self-esteem list and can add to it daily. The more we love ourselves, the closer we are to our higher self.

*

*I am
becoming my own
best friend.*

*

Form—an unfolding creation

Spirit is the energy of the universe, the higher self. Form is the physical world. When our spirit decides to manifest as physical form, we choose a life situation and create a body in accordance with what will best serve and teach us in this lifetime. Ultimately, our goal is to create a form that can do everything our spirit wants to do easily and beautifully. However, the physical world still exists at a relatively primitive level of creation when compared to the consciousness of our spirits. It takes time to manifest form. So we must have patience and love for the unfolding creative process.

*

I *respect*
and love my form as
my creation.

*

Remembering who we are

After we are born we forget who we really are and why we came here. We take on the "survival consciousness" of the physical world and we get lost in the world of form. We lose touch with our true power and our spiritual origin. Life becomes a tremendous struggle to find meaning and satisfaction. More and more we are remembering our connection to the divine and beginning to feel the presence of the higher power in our lives.

*

*I am a
beautiful spirit, creating a
beautiful form.*

*

We have everything we need

We can learn to live in the world of form—our physical bodies, personalities and physical surroundings—without being attached to it. We can have everything the world has to offer, yet be willing to let go of it when we need to. Because the universe within us is rich and powerful, we come to know intuitively that we have everything we need.

*

*I can let go
and trust because I know
I have everything
I need within.*

*

Match your spirit

The first step in the process of consciously transforming your form to match your spirit is to be able to recognize and feel both the consciousness of your spirit and the consciousness of your form. It's a bit like living with two people inside of you. Spirit may want to race ahead, so it has to learn to go at the pace the form can handle.

*

*My spirit and
form are developing at a
harmonious pace.*

*

Integrate your form and spirit

Love and accept both aspects of yourself—form *and* spirit. They are both beautiful and vital parts of you. Without your spirit you wouldn't be alive and without your form you wouldn't be able to exist in the physical world. You'd be existing in some other realm of consciousness. The basic key to integrating spirit and form is learning to listen to your intuition and act on it.

*

I love and
accept both my body and
my spirit.

*

Create a balance within

Sit comfortably with your back straight. Close your eyes. Relax your body completely. Imagine there is a long cord from the base of your spine extending down through the floor into the earth. This is called a grounding cord. Now imagine that the energy of the earth is flowing up through this cord, through all parts of your body, and out through the top of your head. Now imagine that the energy of the cosmos is flowing in through the top of your head, through your body, down through the grounding cord and your feet, and into the earth. Feel both these flows going in different directions and mixing harmoniously in your body. This creates a balance which will increase your sense of well-being, your power of manifestation.

*

I am
grounded and
centered.

*

Learning to channel your
higher self

Almost any form of meditation will eventually take you to an experience of yourself as source, or your "higher self." If you are not sure what this experience is, just continue to practice relaxation, visualization, and affirmation. Eventually you will start to experience certain moments during your meditation when there is a shift in your consciousness and you feel as though things are really working. You may feel energy flowing through you, or a warm, radiant glow in your body. You are beginning to channel the energy of your higher self.

*

I am
more and more in touch with
my higher self.

*

Be patient with yourself

When you first become aware of the experience of your higher self, you may be feeling strong, clear, and creative at one moment, and then be thrown back into confusion and insecurity at the next moment. This seems to be a natural part of the process. At these times it is really important to love yourself while you are feeling these extremes.

*

I

trust my own

process.

*

You have a friend

Each one of us has all the wisdom and knowledge we will ever need right within us. It is available to us through our intuitive mind. One of the best ways to connect with this higher wisdom is by meeting and getting to know our guide, counselor, imaginary friend, or inner being. This is the highest part of yourself. You can think of it as a person or being whom you can talk to and relate to as a wise and loving friend.

*

*I have
a wise and loving friend
within me.*

*

Meeting an inner guide

Close your eyes and relax deeply. Go to your inner sanctuary. Imagine that you are standing on a path. Start to walk up the path. See in the distance a form coming toward you radiating a clear bright light. As you approach the form, see how it looks, how it is dressed, whether it is male or female. Greet this being, ask its name. Take whatever name comes. Show your guide around your sanctuary. Ask if there is anything he or she would like to say to you. You may ask specific questions. When the experience of being together feels complete, thank your guide. Express your appreciation and ask him or her to meet you again in your sanctuary, whenever you desire.

*

*I am now
in contact with a wise
inner guide.*

*

*Put your inner female
in the guiding position*

Each of us, man or woman, has within us an inner male *and* an inner female. The inner female acts as your intuition, the door to your higher intelligence. Your male listens to her and acts to support her feelings. The true function of male energy is to provide absolute clarity, directness, and a passionate strength based on what the universe inside of you, coming through your female, tells you.

In order to live a harmonious and creative life, you need to have both your inner female and male energies fully developed and functioning correctly together. To fully integrate the inner male and female, you need to put your female, your intuition, in the guiding position.

*

*My inner male
is now acting to support
my inner female.*

*

Shifting from fear to trust

The feminine power, the power of the spirit, is
always within us. It is up to the male energy, the ego,
to determine how we relate to that power. We can
fight it, block it, attempt to control it, try to keep
ourselves separate from it, or we can trust and open
up to it, learn to support it and move with it.
Individually and collectively, we are shifting from a
position of fear and control to a position of surrender and trust of the intuitive.

*

My inner male totally
supports, loves, and expresses
my female intuition.

*

Wholeness within

We may not realize that the basic functions of feminine and masculine energies exist in each person. We usually tend to associate male and female energies with their respective body types. From this perspective each person would be only half a person, dependent on the other half for its very existence. As we cannot live effectively in the world without the full range of masculine and feminine energies, each sex has felt helplessly dependent on the other for its very survival. Now, as we are becoming aware of both male and female qualities within us, a deep sense of wholeness can emerge for each individual.

*

I accept both
the masculine and feminine
energies within me;
I feel whole.

*

Expressing power directly

Our female power cannot move directly into the physical world without the support of our male action. Without it, our power is suppressed and must come out indirectly through manipulative patterns or physical symptoms or in sudden un-focused ways—emotional outbursts, even acts of violence. As we practice stating our feelings and needs directly, the need to manipulate falls away and we begin to feel our inherent power.

*

*I now
acknowledge and express
my power directly.*

*

Changing old views

We are changing our way of looking at the world. In our culture, we have used our male energy, our ability to think and act, to suppress and control our feminine intuition, rather than to support and express her. I call this traditional use of the male energy the "old" male, and it exists equally in men and women. Now we can begin to use our male energy in a different way by supporting and listening to our feminine intuition.

*

*I now
use my male energy to express
my intuitive guidance.*

*

Nurturing from within

Traditionally, men have been disconnected from their female energy, thereby disconnected from life, power, and love.

Men have been out there in the world secretly feeling helpless, alone, and empty, although they must pretend to be in control and powerful. They seek nurturing and inner connection through women, but as they connect with their own inner female, they receive her incredible love from within themselves.

*

*My inner female
is nurturing me with
incredible love.*

*

Support from within

Traditionally, women have been in touch with their female energy—intuition and feelings—but they haven't backed her up with their male energy. Many have not acknowledged what they know inside. They have acted as if they were powerless when they are really very powerful. They have sought external support and validation from men. As women claim their inner male and allow him to support their female energy, they feel both feminine and powerful.

*

My inner male
supports and validates
me.

*

We value ourselves

All of us, men and women alike, have gone after external validation rather than valuing what we know and who we are. As we learn to balance the female intuition with male action we move from a state of helplessness to a state of power. We then are no longer dependent on validation from others because we are giving it to ourselves.

*

I
value who
I *am.*

*

Validating yourself

Here is an exercise to help you begin appreciating and validating yourself:

Stand in front of a mirror and look directly in your eyes. In a clear, strong voice make this statement to yourself, "*(your first name)*, one thing I really like about you is . . ." and complete the sentence with something that you appreciate about yourself. It could be a quality of your personality, an aspect of your appearance, or something you've done that you feel proud of. Repeat this process at least ten times, mentioning a different positive attribute each time.

If possible, do this exercise every day for at least a week, and once a week after that.

*

I
like
myself.

*

Your relationship with yourself

In "old world" relationships, the focus was on the other person and on the relationship itself. You communicated for the purpose of trying to get the other person to understand you, to give you more of what you needed. In "new world" relationships, the main focus is on building your relationship with yourself and the universe. You communicate your feelings primarily in order to keep your channel clear, so the life force can keep flowing freely through you.

*

I am now
building a loving relationship
with myself and the
universe.

*

No need to sacrifice

Most people believe that sacrifice and compromise are necessary to preserve a relationship. This is based on a misunderstanding of the nature of the universe. The universe is loving and abundant, and we can all receive everything we need without sacrifice. As we learn to feel and express our needs honestly and clearly to ourselves and to our loved ones, we naturally begin to listen more deeply to the needs of others. On the surface there often seem to be conflicts between our needs and those of others, but with patience and honesty we will discover an underlying truth in which each person can have his/her needs fulfilled.

*

*I express
my needs honestly, listen to
the needs of others, and look
for the deepest truth.*

*

Loving all parts
of ourselves

It is important to accept and experience all of our feelings, including the so-called negative ones, without attempting to change them. At the same time we can create a new point of view about ourselves by embracing and loving all parts of ourselves, not just the parts we already like. As we embrace and express our feelings, we create an intimate and loving relationship with ourselves.

*

I accept
and experience all
my feelings.

*

Express yourself directly

If you are always waiting to be, do, or have what you want, your energy becomes blocked. Your body may reflect this in excess weight or other physical problems. Express yourself directly. Set clear boundaries with other people and do what you need to do to take good care of yourself. Energy will then move freely through your body and this circulation will dissolve any excess weight. The more you are willing to be yourself, the less you'll need to use food as a substitute nurturer. You will be receiving the natural nurturing of the universe.

*

*It is healthy
to express myself clearly
and directly.*

*

Reclaiming our power

When we suppress our natural power to express ourselves and make choices, allowing people to have undue power over us, we feel helpless and victimized. This makes us angry. Because we are frightened of our anger, we tend to suppress it, deadening our other emotions as well. For many people who are becoming more conscious, getting in touch with anger is a very positive sign. It means we are reclaiming our power.

*

As I feel
my anger, I reclaim
my power.

*

Mastery of our lives

When feeling angry, take whatever practical steps are necessary in order to take care of yourself, express your needs, or set your boundaries. But don't focus excessively on the external problems. Instead allow yourself to recognize that it is the loss of your power you feel angry about. As we get more in touch with our power and express it directly and assertively, we no longer feel helpless and angry. Rather, we accept mastery over our own lives.

*

I am
the master of
my life.

*

Expressing anger safely

People are often very frightened of their anger. They feel it will cause them to do something harmful. If you have this fear, create a safe situation where you can express your anger, alone or with a trusted therapist or friend. Allow yourself to talk angrily, shout, hit pillows, whatever you feel like. Once you've done this in a safe environment, you will have released some of the charge, and you can look underneath the anger to find what you need to do to take better care of yourself. Like any emotion, anger is a valuable tool, teaching us who we are and how we feel.

*

*I am now
creating safe ways and places
to express my anger.*

*

Learn to assert yourself

You transform your anger into personal power by learning to assert yourself. Learn to ask for what you want and do what you want to do without being unduly influenced by other people. When you stop giving your power away to other people, you won't feel the same kind of anger anymore. Instead you will feel clear, strong, and honest.

*

*Today
I say what I want
to say and do what
I want to do.*

*

Look for the hurt child

If you are a person who has felt and expressed a lot of anger in your life, you can now look for the hurt that is underneath it and express those feelings. You no longer need to use anger as a defense mechanism to avoid being vulnerable. In order to heal your anger, get in touch with the hurt child within you. Learn to love, nurture, and protect that little child.

*

*It is
safe for me to be
vulnerable.*

*

Express hurt feelings directly

Hurt is an expression of vulnerability. We tend to mask it with defensiveness and blame. It is important to express feelings of hurt directly and if possible, in a non-blaming way. "I felt really hurt when you didn't ask me to go with you," as opposed to "You don't care about my feelings."

Risking the exposure of our true feelings, even hurt or sad feelings, can be scary, but it creates the openness, sharing, and intimacy we crave.

*

I am
*embracing and expressing my
vulnerability.*

*

Allow yourself to grieve

Grief is an intense form of sadness related to the death or ending of something. It is very important to allow ourselves to grieve fully and not to cut this process short. It can sometimes last a long time, or recur periodically for a very long time. Accept it and give yourself as much support as you need whenever grief comes up. It is a paradox that we cannot truly release or end anything unless we grieve for it. The tears move through us, wash us clean, and create the space for something new.

*

As I
allow myself to grieve,
I heal my sadness and create
space for the new.

*

A new level of surrender

Sometimes hurt feelings and grief lead to hopelessness. Hopelessness can lead to surrender. When you feel hopeless, your ego is giving up and you are recognizing that none of your old patterns are working. As you allow yourself to really give up and feel the hopelessness completely, it will be followed by a new level of surrender to the universe, which brings peace and new hope.

*

I am
surrendering to the
universe.

*

Small things first

If you are just beginning to learn how to trust and follow your intuition, you probably don't want to leap off a building and hope that you can fly. It is important that you take small steps first. Practice following your intuition in everyday things, trusting your gut feelings moment by moment and acting on them as best you can. As you learn to trust yourself in smaller matters, you will build power and confidence to take bigger risks and deal with the larger issues in your life successfully.

*

*Step by step
I am building trust in myself
and in the universe.*

*

M A Y   2 3

Money is a reflection

Money is a reflection of the energy moving through your channel. The better you learn to operate in the world based on trust in your intuition, the stronger your channel will be and the more money you will have. The money in your life is based on your ability to listen to your inner guidance and risk acting on it. It flows in an easy, effortless, and joyful way because there is no sacrifice involved. You're no longer attached to it. Instead, you can experience the joy of learning how to follow the energy of the universe. Money is just an extra bonus in the process.

*

As I
trust myself, money comes
to me easily.

*

Balance your checkbook

When it comes to money, balance is as important as in every other area of our lives. If you have been very careless and casual about money, or have denied the existence or importance of money, you may need to pay more attention to the details of handling it. Learn to balance your checkbook and follow a budget. If you see these practices as helping you to build your channel for money, you will find them interesting. They won't hinder your enjoyment, but will open the way for more energy and money to flow through your life.

*

*I enjoy
managing money carefully
and successfully.*

*

Loosen up!

If you've always saved your money and been very careful about spending it, you need to learn to spend more impulsively based on your intuition. Spend on the basis of a gut feeling of wanting something. Loosen up! You deserve it! If you follow your intuition, you won't end up broke. In fact, it will create more prosperity, abundance, and enjoyment in your life.

*

I *deserve*
to spend my money on things
I *desire*.

*

M A Y   2 6

Taking risks with work
and money

Be willing to take some risks in the areas of work and money. If we do only what we think we *should* do in order to make money and be secure, we won't listen to the intuitive voice that tells us to try something new, to be more creative, or to move on to the next step on our path. When we listen to our intuition and take some risks, we are not alone. The universe will support us and reward us for taking risks on its behalf!

*

The universe
rewards me for trying
new things.

*

Ideal scene

List any fantasies you've had about work, career, or a creative or recreational activity. Write an ideal scene, a description of your perfect job or career as you would like it to be. Write in the present tense with description and detail that make it seem very real. Now, close your eyes and experience how it feels to have your fantasy or ideal scene come true. See yourself having all that you want and notice how your body reacts to this possibility. Remember these feelings as you go through your day, and the steps necessary to make it happen will emerge one by one.

*

My
dreams are coming
true.

*

Have whatever you truly desire

The universe is naturally abundant. Everything you truly need or want is here for the asking. Believe that you can have what you want, truly desire it, and be willing to receive it.

*

I *believe in*
abundance, I *desire*
abundance, I *receive*
abundance.

*

The law of attraction

Energy of a certain quality or vibration tends to attract energy of a similar quality and vibration. Thought and feelings have their own magnetic energy, which attracts energy of a similar nature. We can see this principle at work, for instance, when we accidentally run into someone we've just been thinking of, or happen to pick up a book which contains the perfect information we need at that moment.

*

I am now
attracting everything
I need.

*

Expect the best

When we are negative and fearful, insecure or anxious, we tend to attract the very experiences, situations, or people that we are seeking to avoid. We attract these experiences in order to become conscious of and heal our deepest fears. When we are feeling positive in attitude, expecting and en-visioning pleasure, satisfaction, and happiness, we tend to attract and create people, situations, and events which conform to these expectations. There-fore, the more we are able to imagine and accept our highest good, the more it begins to manifest in our lives, and the more power and freedom we will feel.

*

*Today
I expect pleasure and
satisfaction.*

*

Set monthly goals

Once a month list five or six important goals in your life, things that you would like to be putting your energy into right now, or in the near future. Some of them may be short-term, some may be long-term, but they are the ones you feel most strongly about at the moment. With short-range goals, be realistic; with long-range goals, be expansive and idealistic. They may change from month to month. The purpose of writing your goals is to open up and expand your imagination as well as to help you focus on what things are truly important to you.

*

I

*am expanding my
imagination.*

*

*Money is a symbol of our
creative energy*

Money is a symbol of our creative energy. The more willing and able we are to open to the universe, the more money we will have in our lives. Our ability to earn and spend money abundantly and wisely is based on our ability to be a channel for the universe. The stronger and more open our channel is, the more will flow through it.

*

*My channel
is open and money is flowing
to me.*

*

Get in touch with
your fantasies

Most people do have some sense of what they would love to be doing, but this feeling is often repressed and is experienced only in the form of some wildly impractical fantasy. Get in touch with your fantasies. Observe and explore thoroughly your most incredible fantasy. There is truth in your desire, even if it seems impossible. It is telling you something about who you really are and what you want to be doing.

*

I enjoy
my fantasies and look for the
truth within them.

*

Learning and teaching,
work and play

The work you do is a learning experience. I teach workshops, not because I have mastered the information and I am the teacher and you are the student, but because I love to share myself in this way. This sharing deepens my learning experience. There is no difference between learning and teaching. No difference between work and play. It all blends into one totally integrated, balanced experience.

*

In my
life, work and play are
the same.

*

Do what you really love

The more you are willing to trust yourself and take risks to follow your inner guidance, the more money you will have. The universe will pay you to be yourself and do what you really love. For example, you earn money by using your creative energy. You may trade some of that money to me in exchange for the energy I put into writing this book or leading a workshop. The creative energy of the universe in all of us is limitless and readily available. The same is true of money.

*

*The universe
is now paying me to do what I
really love.*

*

Imagine a fabulous career

Get comfortable. Close your eyes. Breathe deeply, relaxing your body and your mind. Imagine you are doing exactly what you want in your life. You have a fabulous career that is fun and fulfilling. You are doing what you've always fantasized about doing and getting a tremendous sum of money for it. You feel relaxed, energized, creative, and powerful. You follow your intuition from moment to moment and are richly rewarded for it. You are doing exactly what you want to be doing.

*

I am
receiving plenty of money
for doing exactly what I
want to do.

*

You are always taken care of

Know that your money is not really yours, but belongs to the universe. You act as a caretaker or steward for money, using it only as directed to use it by your own intuition. There is no fear of loss when you know that you are always taken care of.

*

I care for the
universe's money and the
universe cares for me.

*

Giving and receiving

The universe is made up of pure energy, the nature of which is to move and flow. When we tune into the rhythm of the universe, we are able to give and receive freely, knowing that we never really lose anything, but constantly gain. When we give our energy, we make space for more to flow into us. As we give, we also receive.

*

I *now*
give and receive
freely.

*

Stay open to that flow

Sometimes when we find ourselves fearful, insecure, worried, or believing in scarcity, we cut off the
wonderful flow of energy from the universe. The
abundant energy of the universe flows to us in many
forms: love, affection, appreciation, material possessions, and friendship, to name a few.

It is important to keep our consciousness open to
receiving all the blessings the universe has for us.

*

I *am open*
to receive universal energy in
all its forms.

*

Giving is fun

The more we have given to ourselves, the more we have to give to others. When we find that place within ourselves that is giving, we begin to create an outward flow. Giving to others comes not from a sense of sacrifice, self-righteousness, or spirituality, but for the pure pleasure of it, because it's fun. Giving can only come from a full, loving space.

*

*As I give
to myself, it is fun to give
to others.*

*

The outflow-inflow principle

As we outflow our loving energy, we make room for more and more to flow into us. And the more you share of yourself, the more you seem to get from the world, because of the outflow-inflow principle. As you outflow, you create a space into which something must inflow. Giving becomes its own reward. Remember always that you can't continue to give unless you are equally open to receiving. Giving also includes giving to yourself.

*

As
I *give*, I
receive.

*

J U N E 1 1

Give love and appreciation

Sit down right now and make a list of people to whom you would like to give love and appreciation, and think of a way that you can do so to each one within the next week. This could be by touching, making a phone call, sending a gift, giving money, anything that makes you feel good. Practice speaking more words of thanks, appreciation, and admiration to people.

*

I *give*
love and appreciation
to others.

*

A *constant choice*

Life is the choice to follow the flow of energy within us. Death is the choice to block this flow of life energy. We are faced with this life or death choice every moment of our lives. When we choose not to follow our intuitive promptings, we close off our channel. We receive less energy, and our body begins to deteriorate. But as we follow our intuition, we open up, we receive more energy, and our body regenerates.

*

I
choose
life.

*

Strengthen your body

A strong body is not created just by eating certain foods, doing certain exercises, or following some-body's rules or ideas. It is created by trusting your intuition and learning to follow its direction. When your inner guidance tells you what to eat, how to exercise, or anything else, trust that this advice will create a strong and flexible body.

*

*My intuition
knows what my body
needs.*

*

Your body knows

The way to a beautiful, strong, healthy body is to start by trusting yourself right now. Let go of the struggle and surrender to your body's needs. Your intuition will tell you what to eat. It may direct you to exercise vigorously, in which case you'll enjoy it, or it may tell you to slow down and rest. It may tell you to stay in bed all day, or it may tell you to get up early. There are no rigid rules. Your body knows perfectly well what's good for it.

*

*I now
surrender to my body's
needs.*

*

Trust yourself

People generally react with fear when I suggest that they trust themselves and follow their body's needs. They are afraid they will stay in bed all day, eat chocolates, and get fat. If you have food addictions, be sure to get counseling and group support to discover the underlying causes and to stop the addictive behavior. Practice listening to and following what your body *really* wants. Trust yourself. You will start to look and feel as your spirit is—alive and energized, beautiful and young.

*

*I trust
my body, I trust
myself.*

*

Remember to check inside

For me, it is a constant discipline to remember to go back inside to connect with my intuition. I remind myself regularly during the day to do this. If I find myself getting lost in my outer activities, I check back inside to see if I am being true to my feelings. This keeps the flow of the universe moving through me.

*

I *remember*
to check with my
intuition.

*

Facing our unconsciousness

None of us are fully enlightened yet, so as we risk expressing ourselves more freely and honestly, some of what comes out will be unpolished, distorted, foolish, or thoughtless. As we learn to act on our inner feelings, all the ways we've blocked ourselves in the past come to awareness and are cleared out. In this process, we have to be willing to face our lack of awareness without self-judgment, but with compassion for ourselves. In this way we can clear our distortions and become more conscious beings.

*

*I accept
and express the way
I feel.*

*

Acknowledging our need

It is the hidden, unacknowledged needs that cause us to seem needy. They don't come out directly, but are expressed indirectly, or telepathically. Other people feel them and back away from us because they intuitively know they can't help us if we aren't acknowledging our need for help. It's paradoxical that we actually become stronger as we recognize and acknowledge our own needs and ask for help directly. People find it easier to give to us, and we feel more and more whole.

*

I am
recognizing and expressing
my needs.

*

Speaking truthfully

When I communicate truthfully and directly, saying everything I really want to say, it doesn't seem to matter too much how other people respond. They may not do or say exactly what I'd like, but I feel so clear and empowered from taking care of myself, that it's easier to let go of the result. If I am honest and vulnerable in expressing my feelings to my lover, family, and friends, I don't end up with hidden needs or resentment.

*

Today I take care
of myself by communicating
my truth directly.

*

Finding our own fulfillment

Other people are seldom able to fulfill our needs consistently, so we become disappointed and frustrated. We either try to change others, which never works, or resign ourselves to accept less than we really want. When another person disappoints us, it may be a message that it's time to look to ourselves for fulfillment and satisfaction. We may need to express our honest feelings to the other person clearly and simply, and then let go and look within for guidance about what we need to do for ourselves.

*

My needs
are filled from the
universe within.

*

The stronger the attraction,
the stronger the mirror

I have found that when I am willing to trust and follow my energy it leads me into relationships with people from whom I have the most to learn. The stronger the attraction, the stronger the mirror. My energy will always lead me to the most intense learning situation. I don't need to enter or stay in a relationship that is not good for me, but if I choose to leave I can still acknowledge the gift and the teaching I received.

*

I accept
my relationships as
my teachers.

*

You are unique

I foresee a time when each person can truly be a unique entity with his or her own free-flowing style of expression. Each relationship will be a unique connection between two beings, taking its individual form and expression. No stereotypes will be possible because each one of us is so individual when we follow the flow of our own energy.

*

*I am
a unique entity;
each of my relationships is
unique.*

*

Children are powerful,
spiritual beings

I have met a lot of parents who, now that they have become more aware, feel much guilt and sadness in looking back at how they've raised their children. Remember that children are powerful, spiritual beings who are responsible for their own lives. They chose you as a parent so they could learn the things they needed to learn in this lifetime.

*

I take responsibility
for my life choices and I allow
others to take responsibility
for theirs.

*

Children copy what we do

Children do not need us to behave perfectly. They do need us to create an example of how to live effectively in the world of form. They need our imperfect "humanness." As we live our lives, they watch us, notice how we express our feelings and our dreams, and they imitate us. Being very perceptive and pragmatic, they copy what we actually do, not what we say. The more we are our true selves, the more we give them permission to be their true selves.

*

As I learn
to be myself, I inspire others
to be themselves.

*

Support their power

Many people hold an underlying attitude that children are helpless or untrustworthy and that parents are completely responsible for controlling and molding them. Children, of course, pick up this attitude and reflect it in their behavior—acting more helpless than they really are, or behaving in an untrustworthy manner. If you recognize children as powerful, spiritually mature beings, they will act accordingly, as will your friends, your lovers, and you. Affirm these positive attributes daily for yourself and everyone around you.

*

I recognize
others as powerful, capable,
responsible beings.

*

Allow yourself safety
and support

We have to learn to use our powerful male energy to listen to, trust, and support our female energy. This allows us the safety and support to risk opening and expressing the full range of our feelings . We can be sensitive, receptive, and vulnerable, and are at the same time, stronger, more alive, and more powerful than ever before.

*

The more I
support and trust my feelings,
the stronger and more open
I am.

*

Let your power shine

In the traditional female role, a woman learns to use her male energy to deny and suppress her natural female power. This leaves her helpless, dependent on men, emotionally unbalanced, and able to express her power only indirectly through manipulation. She may be afraid that if men found out how powerful she really is, they would abandon her. So she carefully keeps her power hidden. As we come to trust and take care of ourselves, it feels safer to risk being a powerful, creative person.

*

*It is
safe for me to be
powerful.*

*

Express positive male power

Many very conscious men have chosen to connect deeply with their feminine energy and yet, in doing so, have disconnected from their male. They have rejected the old macho image and have no other concept of male energy to relate to. These men are usually afraid of their male energy. They feel it will burst forth with the old mindlessness and violence they equate with maleness. Thus they lose the positive, assertive male qualities as well. As men begin to find the balance of the female and male energies within, they will realize that their strength and assertiveness is being safely and accurately guided by their intuition.

*

It is
safe for me to express my
male energy.

*

*We are becoming more
responsible*

We are now learning to rely on and validate ourselves instead of abandoning the responsibility and
depending on someone else to do it for us. Because
this dependency is a deep-seated pattern that has
endured for centuries, it takes time to change it. The
key is for us to just keep listening to, trusting in, and
acting on our deepest feelings, while loving and
approving of ourselves as much as we can.

*

*I accept the
responsibility of listening to
and loving myself.*

*

Create a treasure map

A treasure map is an actual physical picture of a desired goal. It works along the same lines as a blueprint for a building. You can draw it, paint it, or make a collage with magazine pictures and photos. Simple, childlike treasure maps are very effective and fun to do. Basically, it should show you in your ideal scene with your goal fully realized. Include all the elements without getting too complicated. Use lots of color. Include some symbol of the infinite which has meaning and power for you. Put affirmations on your treasure map. This creative process is a powerful physical step toward manifesting your goal.

*

This or something
better is now manifesting for
me in totally satisfying
and harmonious ways.

*

*
**

Summer

**
*

Attachment to goals

If you have a great deal of attachment to a particular goal, it may interfere with your ability to manifest it. Often, when there is a strong attachment to something, there is a great deal of fear underneath—fear of not getting what we need.

It's perfectly okay to creatively visualize something to which you have a lot of attachment. If it doesn't work out, realize that your own inner conflict may be sending out conflicting messages. Relax and accept your feelings. Understand that resolving the inner conflict is probably an important part of growth for you and a wonderful opportunity to look more closely at your own attitudes about life.

*

*I relax
and accept my
feelings.*

*

*Blocked energy can
be released*

Creative power has to filter through our beliefs, attitudes, emotions, and habits. The more negative and constricted our beliefs and patterns are, the more they block the creative energy. Most people hope that by ignoring negativity, it will go away, but the reverse is actually true. Through recognizing, acknowledging, and experiencing it, the blocked energy can be released. You are then free to replace it with positive beliefs and attitudes.

*

*Through recognizing
and acknowledging my blocks,
I release and
clear them.*

*

A *clearing process*

Here is a basic clearing process that you can use to clear out negative beliefs in order to attain a goal. First state your goal in the form of an affirmation. Second, write "The reasons I can't have what I want are:", and then start listing every thought that comes into your head. Third, decide which of the negative statements have the most power over you, and make a mark by those. Write an affirmation to counteract each one. Meditate on these affirmations every day along with your original goal.

*

*I am now
clearing my negative
beliefs.*

*

Declare your independence

The key to independence lies in knowing that at every moment, in every instance, we are creating our life. The more we acknowledge this truth, the more power and freedom we experience.

Rather than blaming ourselves for the things we do not like in our life, we now realize we are manifesting our reality and have the power to change it.

Our life is a reflection of what we believe we deserve. As we deepen our acceptance of and open ourselves to the infinite love of the universe, a new power flows through us, releasing us from the bondage of our old way of life.

*

I feel the
freedom and power to create
the life I desire.

*

Let go and ask

In certain situations you may try to do affirmations and find that you simply can't do them, or, if you do, it doesn't feel like you're accomplishing anything. In that case, it may be time for you to let go of what you were trying to do. Get in touch with your inner guidance and ask what to do next. You have access to an everpresent resource within that will guide you to your highest good.

*

*I am
asking my higher self
for guidance.*

*

*Learning to follow
the spirit within*

I am learning to follow the spirit within me, wherever it wants to take me. Every time I check in, feeling the energy inside me and letting it direct me, I find this is a wonderful way to live. When I do this, I experience joy, power, love, peace, and excitement.

*

*I am
learning to follow the spirit
within me.*

*

The choice is simple,
life or death

Every time I follow my inner voice, I feel more life and energy. Every time I go against it, I feel the struggle in my body. If I continue to push myself past what my body wants, I become increasingly tired and lifeless. The choice is simple, life or death. Moment to moment become keenly aware of what makes you feel most alive. Start a list of these "alive" times and consciously choose these activities for yourself.

*

Every time
I follow my inner voice I
feel more alive.

*

*Notice how you look
and feel*

Get in a comfortable position. Close your eyes.
Breathe deeply. Relax your body and your mind.
Recall a recent situation in which you did not do
what you wanted to do. Replay this scene in your
mind. Notice how you looked and felt physically,
emotionally, and spiritually. Now go back and see
yourself doing exactly what you'd like in that situation. Notice how your body feels. Notice how you
look, and how you feel about yourself. Spend a few
minutes feeling what it's like to trust yourself and
act on your desires.

*

*I trust
myself and I act on
that trust.*

*

Keep a journal

Keep a journal of some of the decisions you make during the day. Notice when you do what you want, when you choose not to, and for what reasons. For example, you may choose to go to a party when you really want to stay home. Do you push yourself to work hard even if you are not feeling well? Do you hold back from expressing your ideas, feelings, or creative impulses out of fear of criticism?

Write how you feel about the choices you made. Notice how you felt physically and emotionally. Be careful not to judge or criticize yourself for any of your choices. Cultivate an attitude of compassionate observation so you can learn what works for you and what doesn't.

*

*Today I pay
attention to how I feel about the
choices I make.*

*

Achieving balance

The feminine (spiritual) energy is a powerful force that moves us toward union and oneness. The masculine energy (or ego) defines our individuality. Both are equally necessary and important for living successfully in the physical world.

As we learn to trust, honor, and express our feminine and masculine energies in harmony with one another, we feel our oneness with all of life and at the same time we appreciate and respect our uniqueness. We achieve balance in every aspect of our lives.

*

*I am a unique
individual and I am one
with the universe.*

*

Our inner female will
guide us perfectly

If we don't pay conscious attention to our inner
female (feminine energy) in our waking life, she
attempts to reach us through our dreams, our
emotions, and our physical body. She is the source
of higher wisdom within us, and if we learn to listen
carefully to her moment by moment, she will guide
us perfectly.

*

My inner
female is my
guide.

*

*Ask your female voice
what she wants*

Close your eyes and contact your female, intuitive voice; ask her what she wants. Is there a gift she desires, or something she wants to say or do? When you have received her communication, see your new male as supporting her desires. See him taking whatever action necessary to honor her needs and desires. When you open your eyes, do your best to follow whatever your female wants you to do.

*

*My male energy
supports and acts on the
desires of my inner
female.*

*

*The lovers they are
meant to be*

The power of the feminine energy is on the rise in our world. As she emerges within us and we acknowledge and surrender to her, the old controlling male within us is transformed. He re-emerges, birthed through the female as the "new male," the powerful male who goes all out in his trust and love for her. He grows to become her equal in power, so that they can be the lovers they are meant to be.

*

*My male and
female energies are uniting
as lovers.*

*

The birth of the new male

I believe that the new male has been truly birthed in our consciousness only within the last few years. Before that we had little experience in our bodies of the true male energy. Our only concept of the male was the "old male," an energy completely divorced from the feminine. The birth of the new male is synonymous with the birth of the new age. The new world is being built within us and mirrored around us as the new male (form) emerges in all his glory from the feminine power (spirit).

*

My inner
male is growing stronger
every day.

*

*Ask for images of
male and female*

Get in a comfortable position, close your eyes, relax your body. Now bring to your mind an image that represents your inner female. Take a look at your female and get a sense or a feeling of what she represents to you. Ask her if she has anything she would like to say to you and/or ask her any questions you may have. Once you have allowed yourself to receive her communication, take a deep breath and release her from your mind. Come back to a quiet, still place. Do the same process with the male. Then ask for the images of both male and female to come to you. See how they relate to one another. Ask them if they have anything they would like to communicate to each other or to you. Then once again take a deep breath and release these images from your mind. Come back to a still, quiet place.

*

*I am
in touch with my inner
male and female.*

*

Our own special path

When instead of following our own intuitive know-ingness, we follow the behavior we have observed in others or attempt to follow the rules and regula-tions laid down by others, we move in ways that are counter to our own natural flow. This means we are not acting on what *we* know. We are not saying and doing what we really feel. We have stopped listen-ing to the signals our body gives us about food, rest, and love. As we learn to pay attention, we begin to see the difference between old messages from oth-ers and our own natural signals. The more we listen to and trust ourselves, the more our own special path unfolds magically before us.

*

*Today
I follow my own
path.*

*

Our body is our primary creation

Our body is the vehicle we have created to express us in the physical world. It's like a semi-formed piece of clay that molds itself to show the patterns of energy moving through it. The body is our primary feedback mechanism which can show us what is and isn't working about our ways of thinking, expressing, and living. As we live our truth more fully and freely, our body grows healthier, stronger, and more beautiful.

*

My body
beautifully expresses who
I am.

*

A *solid base of trust*

We are unafraid to the same degree that we experience the presence of the universe in our own body. Every time we open ourselves up to more power, more of the old fear gets flushed to the surface and released. In the healing process we experience alternating states of power and fear. Gradually, a solid base of trust is established within us. The more light we allow within us, the brighter the world we live in will be.

*

*I am
building a solid base of
trust within.*

*

What I am right now

If we pretend to be more enlightened than we really are, we will miss an opportunity to heal ourselves. Admitting our limitations can make us feel vulnerable, yet it is very freeing.

We just have to be ourselves as we are now, accepting the mixture of enlightened awareness and human limitation that is in each of us. Through this self-acceptance, we find a deep peace and self-love.

*

Today
I accept myself as
I am.

*

Forgiving and releasing

Write down the names of everyone in your life toward whom you feel or have felt resentment, hurt, or anger. Write down what they did to you and what you resent them for. Then close your eyes, relax, and visualize each person. Explain to them what you have felt angry about, and explain the hurt beneath the anger. Tell them that now you are going to do your best to dissolve and release all constricted energy between you. Give them a blessing and say, "I forgive you and release you. Go your own way and be happy."

*

*I am
now forgiving and releasing
everyone.*

*

Put yourself first

What does it mean to take care of yourself? It means trusting and following your intuition, taking time to listen to all of your feelings including the feelings of the child within you that is sometimes hurt or scared. It means responding with caring, love, and appropriate action. It means putting your needs first and trusting that everyone else's needs will get taken care of, that everything that needs to be done will be handled. It means trusting that the universe is looking after each and every one of us.

*

*Today
I am listening and responding
to my own needs.*

*

We are spontaneous beings

Any normal child who has a reasonably positive environment has a body filled with beauty and vitality. The natural life energy of the universe flows freely through, unimpeded by negative habits.

In a supportive environment, we are totally spontaneous beings. We eat when we are hungry, fall asleep when we are tired, and express exactly what we feel, so the energy doesn't get blocked. We are constantly renewed and revitalized by our own natural energy.

*

*I am
a natural, spontaneous
being.*

*

Young children are our
clearest mirrors

Young children are often our clearest mirrors because as intuitive beings, they are tuned in on a feeling level and respond honestly to every situation. They haven't learned to cover up their feelings yet. When we as adults do not speak or behave according to what we are actually feeling, children pick up the discrepancy immediately and react to it. Watching their reactions can help us become more aware of our own suppressed feelings.

*

I am
becoming more aware of
my feelings.

*

Children need honesty

Many parents think they have to protect their children from their (the parents') confusion or so-called negative feelings. They think that being a good parent means always maintaining a certain role: being patient, loving, wise, and strong. But in fact, children need honesty. They need to see a human being experience the full range of human emotion and be honest about it. This gives children permission to support and love themselves as natural and truthful beings.

*

Today
I am giving the gift
of my honesty.

*

Forgiving yourself

Write down the names of everyone you can think of in your life whom you feel you have hurt and what you did to them. Close your eyes, relax, and imagine each person. Tell him or her what you did and ask them to forgive you and give you their blessing. Then picture them doing so. When you have finished this process, write "I forgive myself and absolve myself of all guilt, here and now, and forever!"

*

I
*forgive myself
completely.*

*

Recognizing old patterns

We begin very early to develop habits that run counter to our natural energy, habits that are designed to help us survive in the neurotic world in which we find ourselves. We pick up these patterns from our families, friends, teachers, and the community in general. Eventually we begin to see that these habits are no longer serving us. Through becoming aware of them, we take the first and most important step toward releasing them.

*

It is
safe for me to let go
of old habits.

*

Transforming the darkness
into light

When you recognize and feel the futility of an old pattern, it is about to change. Shortly you will begin to respond differently to things, and in a more positive way. Enlightenment of the form happens through a miraculous process. As the ego surrenders to the universe, the spirit penetrates every cell of the body, transforming the darkness into light.

*

As I
surrender to the source, I feel
spirit transforming me.

*

Get the message

If there are problems in your life, it means the universe is trying to get your attention. It's saying "Hey, there's something you need to be aware of, something that needs to be changed here." If you don't pay attention, the problems will intensify, until you finally get the message and start to listen more carefully to your inner guidance. If you learn to pay attention to the small signals, you will learn from them and your problems will be solved with ease.

*

I listen
to the small signals and
learn from them.

*

Ask the universe for help

It does not always help to analyze and think about problems with your rational mind. Sometimes it is far more effective to turn to your inner self, to ask the universe for help. Simply sit quietly. Take a few deep breaths and focus your awareness within. Ask your wise inner self, either silently or aloud, for guidance or help in understanding the message. As you get a sense of what feels right, act on this feeling.

*

*My inner self
gives me guidance and
direction.*

*

Create the space for intimacy

As I learn to love myself, I automatically receive the love and appreciation from others that I desire. My willingness to be intimate with my own deep feelings creates the space for intimacy with another. As I feel the power of the universe flowing through me, I create a life of passion and fulfillment which I can share with others.

*

I am
willing to be intimate with
my own deep feelings.

*

The quality of love

Close your eyes. Deeply relax. When you feel relaxed and energized say, "I now call forth the quality of love." Feel the energy of love coming to you, or out from someplace inside of you, filling you up and radiating out from you. Remain for a few minutes experiencing this feeling. Then if you wish, direct it toward anyone to whom you wish to send a blessing.

*

I *now*
call forth the quality
of love.

*

Creating an abundant world

Poverty on both a personal and worldwide level is supported by our collective belief in scarcity. We deeply fear that there is not enough to go around of whatever we need—money, food, love, energy, or appreciation. As we begin to acknowledge that this is a rich universe with plenty for all of us, we create a world that supports this belief. We are capable of channeling tremendous joy and prosperity into this life.

*

*There is
enough of everything
for everyone.*

*

Exploring our fantasies

At times fantasies can tell us how we really want to be expressing ourselves. We sometimes have a strong sense of what we would like to do, yet we take up a very different career. We feel we need a career that is more practical or will gain the approval of our parents or the world.

In the past we have felt it was impossible to do what we really wanted. We are now seeing that when we do what we really want we gain our own approval. We experience our own vitality and freedom. Today we can risk exploring things that really turn us on.

*

*I now
risk exploring things that
excite me.*

*

Follow the impulse

Follow any impulse that you have in the direction of your true work/play desires. Even if it seems unrealistic, follow the impulse anyway. For example, if you are 65 years old and have always wanted to be a ballet dancer, go to a ballet class and observe. Watch ballet performances. Imagine you are a dancer. At home alone, put on some music and dance freely in whatever way feels good to your body. This will get you in touch with a part of yourself that wants and needs expression. You may end up dancing much more than you thought possible and you may be led to other and different forms of expression that will feel wonderful.

*

I am now
following my creative
impulses.

*

Learning can be fun

The learning process can be full of joy, fun, and excitement. We can experience it as a wonderful adventure. We no longer need to sacrifice and struggle in the moment to have what we want in the future. The journey and the destination become one and the same. Learning new skills, going to school, exploring untried talents—any of these can be fun and fulfilling if you are following your intuition.

*

*My
learning is full of
joy.*

*

Celebrate your gifts

If you are having trouble deciding just what it is that you are supposed to be doing with your life, pay attention to what energizes you, what excites you, what widens your horizons, and brings you joy. Choose to allow your channel to function as it wishes. Energy will flow through you and skills will come easily as the universe moves to support you in the celebration and expression of your gifts.

*

*I express
my gifts easily and
skillfully.*

*

Lives will be transformed

Whether you are washing the dishes, taking a walk, or building a house, if you are doing it with a sense of being where you want to be and doing what you want to be doing, the fullness of that experience will be felt by those around you. They will sense the completeness of your experience and their lives will be transformed to the degree that they are ready to allow the impact of that experience to affect them.

*

My joy
is felt by everyone
around me.

*

You can transform others

If you walk into a room loving yourself, knowing that you are a creative channel, and expressing yourself honestly, everyone in the room can be affected, even though they may not be aware of it. As a direct result of your presence, you will see others become more alive and empowered. It is an incredibly exciting and satisfying experience.

*

*I am one
with my self, a channel
for the universe.*

*

We are not alone

Once we accept the reality of a higher power operating in the universe, channeled through our intuition, it becomes clear that our personal problems, and even world problems, are actually caused by not respecting that intuition. Personal and social problems are a result of fear and the suppression of our intuition.

We are not alone with our problems. We can rely on our intuition as if it were a great and wise friend accompanying us on this journey through life—watching out for us, helping us, loving us. We can practice following our intuition with the certainty that we are loved and cared for.

*

*I am
guided by my higher power
at all times.*

*

Change occurs naturally

If you feel your progress toward your goals is too slow, ask the universe for help. Remind yourself that things will always change in time. Change happens not by forcing it, but by becoming aware of what's not working in your life and being willing to let it go. Change, a dynamic, natural process, is always occurring, even when we're not aware of it.

*

I *allow things*
to change in their own
natural time.

*

Increasing our aliveness

Every time we don't trust ourselves and our inner truth, we decrease our aliveness. Our bodies will reflect this with numbness, pain, and a loss of vitality.

Every time we allow the energy of the universe to move through us by trusting and following our intuition, we increase our sense of aliveness. Our bodies will reflect this with health, beauty, and vitality.

*

*I trust
my inner truth and I feel
vibrantly alive.*

*

Unblock the flow

When we are blocking the flow of energy we begin to experience less and less vitality. As the flow diminishes, our bodies are slow to revitalize. They begin to age and deteriorate. Poor posture, tight jaws, headaches, and backaches are all reflections of chronic energy blocks.

By relaxing and nurturing ourselves, by healing our emotional wounds, by reaching for what gives us joy, we can release these patterns from our lives. In turn, our bodies will experience a new ease and new power.

*

*I relax
and nurture myself;
I open to joy.*

*

Assert yourself consistently

The most important key to creating your perfect body is learning to assert yourself consistently in your life. For example, overweight people may have a pattern of doubting themselves, of being afraid to trust their feelings and act on them. We especially need to learn how to say no to others when we don't want to do something. Overweight people often try to please and take care of others. When our first priority is to please and take care of others, we are denying who we really are and what we really feel. When we are afraid to be true to ourselves, our bodies will always serve us by reflecting these fears, so we can become conscious of them and heal them.

*

Today
I am willing to assert
myself.

*

Take action

The key to asserting yourself is to take action on your feelings and intuition. I have seen people begin to lose weight or become physically healthier simply by doing something they've been afraid to do, or by expressing some feeling they've suppressed. By becoming more assertive, underweight people become more willing to take up space in the world. By continuing to speak and act your truth, you will dissolve blocks and find your proper weight.

*

I now
take action on my
feelings.

*

Risk asserting yourself

At first the prospect of asserting yourself moment to moment can be frightening. We are not used to stating what we need and taking the action necessary to give it to ourselves. It takes a conscious effort for us to tune in to how we feel and to risk doing it. But once you start, you'll want to keep doing it. You will have more energy and look more radiant.

*

It is safe
for me to assert my needs
and feelings.

*

*Balancing weight easily
and naturally*

Once overweight people learn true assertion, they are often able to lose weight easily and naturally, without any type of deprivation. The increased energy circulating in their bodies dissolves the blocked energy and the extra weight gradually melts away. They do not need it for strength or protection so they release it effortlessly.

By the same process of assertion, underweight people release their fear, and are able to take in more life and more nourishment. It becomes safe for them to take up more space. If any particular food plan is needed, they will be intuitively led to an appropriate nutritional consultant and diet.

*

As I trust and
assert my feelings, I create my
perfect body.

*

It is our birthright

We have spent many years believing it is necessary to compromise and sacrifice for others. We have long carried the belief that "you can't have everything." We fear we have no right to our feelings and desires.

It is absolutely our birthright as children of the light to have all the joy, happiness, and abundance in the universe. As we celebrate ourselves, by expressing who we are and how we feel, we draw light and love, not only to ourselves, but to everyone around us.

*

I deserve
love, happiness, and
prosperity.

*

Being a good parent

Our old ideas of parenting usually involved feeling totally responsible for the welfare of our children and following some specific standards of behavior. As you learn to trust yourself and be yourself, you may find that you are violating many of your old rules about what a good parent does. Yet the vibrant energy that is coming through you, your increasing sense of satisfaction in your life, and your trust of yourself and the universe, will do far more to help your children than anything else possibly could.

*

My loved ones
benefit when I trust and
be myself.

*

A U G U S T   1 8

*Those you love will be
positively affected*

As we learn to fulfill our own needs, we are often afraid that our families and friends will suffer. However, the opposite is true. Just as a pebble thrown into a pond sends out ripples, those you love will be positively affected and supported as you grow and evolve. They will change as you change, even if they live far away from you, since all relationships are telepathic. Your growth and transformation will be reflected in others.

*

*As I
grow, everyone
grows.*

*

The dance of life

Female and male, being and doing, receiving and expressing, destroying and creating, grieving and rejoicing—these polarities create the dance of life. Each of us contains within us the full spectrum of life's energies. To the degree that we accept and express all aspects of ourselves, we become whole and conscious channels of the universe.

*

*I am
experiencing and expressing
the dance of life.*

*

The basis of all creation

The union of feminine and masculine energies within the individual is the basis of all creation. Female intuition plus male action equals creativity. The female within says, "I feel this." The inner male says, "I hear your feelings, what would you like me to do?" She says, "I want that." He says, "You want that, okay great, I'll get it for you." And he goes directly to get it for her, trusting that in her desire is the wisdom of the universe.

*

*My feminine
and masculine energies are in
perfect harmony.*

*

Be willing to follow that guidance

The nature of the feminine is wisdom, love, and clear vision expressed through feeling and desire. The masculine energy is all-out risk-taking action, in service to the feminine, much like the chivalrous knight and his lady. Remember now that we are talking about an internal process in each of us, male and female alike. We are not saying that men should let women tell them what to do, but that we each need to let our intuition guide us and then be willing to follow that guidance directly and fearlessly.

*

*I am following
the guidance of my intuition,
directly and fearlessly.*

*

From a place of power

In the past men have desperately needed women to provide them with the nurturing, intuitive, and emotional support they need, and women have been dependent on men to take care of them and provide for them in the physical world. It seems like a perfect arrangement, except for one problem. When you don't feel whole, as an individual, when you feel your survival depends on others, you are constantly afraid of losing them.

We have been struggling with these "old male" and "old female" roles for many generations. So it is wonderful that we are beginning to discover that each of us has all the qualities within to be whole and happy, giving and receiving from a place of power.

*

I

am

whole.

*

The male in women

Both the old male (macho) and the old female (submissive) exist in each sex. A woman who feels caught in the traditional female role has a controlling, macho old male inside of her, suppressing her. She will tend to attract men who mirror this male personality and will reflect it in their behavior toward her. This behavior may range from paternalistic and chauvinistic to verbally or physically abusive, depending on how the woman treats herself and what she believes she deserves. By acknowledging her own internal male she takes the power of healing back into her own hands. As she begins to use her male energy to trust, support, and express her own inner feelings, her self-love will be reflected in her relationships.

*

*My inner
male loves and supports
me.*

*

The female in men

The traditional macho man has been taught to suppress and deny his inner female self, who becomes desperate to be recognized and loved. He will tend to attract women who have a low self-image, who are clinging and needy, or who express their power indirectly through manipulation, little girl cuteness, cattiness, or dishonesty. These women reflect his lack of trust and respect for his inner female by not trusting and respecting themselves. As he begins to recognize them as reflections of his own female, he can begin to love and honor the powerful, nurturing woman inside him.

*

*I trust
and respect my inner
female.*

*

Men will reflect her shift

Once a woman begins to trust and love herself more, and starts to use her internal male energy to support herself, the behavior of men in her life will reflect that shift. They will either change dramatically and continue to change as she does, or they will disappear from her life to be replaced by men who are supportive and appreciative of her, mirroring her new attitude towards herself. I have seen this happen over and over again.

*

*I support
and appreciate
myself.*

*

*Women will mirror
his change*

By opening to and trusting his own feminine nature, a man will find within himself the nurturing, support, and connection he has been lacking. The women in his life will mirror this shift by becoming stronger, more independent, more direct, honest, and more genuinely loving and nurturing.

*

As I
*nurture myself, I am nurtured
by others.*

*

When male and female
are in harmony

I often imagine my male standing behind my female—supporting, protecting, backing her up. For a man the image might be reversed. You might see your female as within or behind you—guiding, empowering, nurturing and supporting you. When male and female energies are in harmony and working together, it is an incredible feeling. One becomes a strong, open, creative channel with power, wisdom, peace, and love flowing through.

*

My male and
female energies are working
in harmony.

*

A *mirror of yourself*

If you know on a deep level that the person you are attracted to is a mirror of yourself, you know that everything that you see in your partner is also in you. The reason you are in relationships is to learn about yourself and deepen your connection with your higher self. Healthy relationships are not based on neediness, but on the passion and excitement of sharing the journey of becoming a whole person.

*

*I learn about
myself through the mirror of
my relationships.*

*

A *love affair with*
the universe

Because many of us have never really learned how to take good care of ourselves, our relationships have been based on trying to get someone else to take care of us. In the past, we have tried to use falling in love to fill up an empty space within us. We are now finding that being alive is a love affair with the universe. Life is a love affair between our inner male and female, between our form and our spirit.

*

I am now
having a love affair with
the universe.

*

Treat yourself the way you want
to be treated

The qualities that women look for in men—strength, power, daring, excitement, romance—need to be developed within themselves. Likewise, men must develop the qualities they look for in women—caring, compassion, nurturing, tenderness, intuitiveness. Imagine how you'd want to be treated by a perfect lover, then begin to treat yourself exactly that way.

*

I treat
myself exactly the way I want
to be treated.

*

Imagine the universe is your lover

Take yourself on a romantic date. Prepare for it as if you were going out with the most loving and exciting partner you can imagine. Take a luxurious hot bath. Dress up in your best clothes. Buy yourself flowers. Have a lovely dinner, or a moonlight stroll. Spend the evening telling yourself how wonderful you are, and anything else that you would like to hear from a lover. Imagine that the universe is your lover giving you everything you want.

*

*The
universe is my
lover.*

*

A powerful force of creation

In our society we have started to recognize the destructive power of the old "macho" male and the impotence of the old "victim" female. While we have begun to validate the importance of our new "intuitive" female, we have tended to label our male energy as "bad." Consequently, we are in danger of disowning a powerful and necessary force of creation which burns within each of us. We must now affirm and reclaim this energy and allow it to flow freely and magnificently through our lives.

*

*The power
of my male energy is flowing
through me.*

*

Embrace the new male

To embrace and express the power of the new male within us, we must allow our spontaneous, active, aggressive male energy to flow freely, knowing that the power of our feminine is in charge, wisely directing us. This requires a deep trust that our inner female knows what she's doing and won't allow anything destructive or harmful to happen.

*

I *trust*
and express my
new male.

*

Uniting the energies

The women I know who are going through the process of uniting their male and female energies seem to become more feminine and beautiful while they are strengthening their male qualities. Men who are surrendering and opening fully to their female energy are actually reconnecting with an inner feminine power which enhances and strengthens their masculine qualities. Far from becoming effeminate, the men I know who are involved in this process seem more secure in their maleness.

*

*As I reconnect with
my inner male and female,
I am more secure
in myself.*

*

Important mirrors

Think of some of the most important women in your life. What are their strongest and most attractive qualities? Be aware that they mirror some aspect of your own female energy, whether you are a man or a woman. Now follow the same process for some of the most important men in your life. If you have trouble seeing that some of the things you admire in others are in you as well, it may be because you have not yet developed these qualities in yourself as strongly as they have, but know that they are there and they can be developed.

*

*I have
all the qualities I admire
in others.*

*

Your channel opens wide

Falling in love is actually a powerful experience of feeling the universe move through you. The other person has become a catalyst that triggers you to open up to the love, beauty, and passion that is within you. Your channel opens wide and the universal energy comes pouring through. You have a blissful moment of enlightenment.

*

I *am*
falling in love
with life.

*

Lovers are special mirrors

As we build and open our channel, more and more energy flows through, more feeling and passion. Certain people attract us very strongly and intensify or deepen our experience of the life force within us. These people are important mirrors for us and they are channels for special energy in our life. Through them we can learn some of the most important teachings life has to offer us.

*

*My lover
is my mirror.*

*

*You receive what you
always wanted*

It is interesting that what we create within us is always mirrored outside of us. This is the law of the universe. When you have built an inner male and female who support and love you, there will always be men and women in your life reflecting this. When you truly give up trying to become whole through others, you end up receiving what you always wanted from others.

*

*The more
I love myself, the more
others love me.*

*

Change old patterns

Take a good look at how external problems reflect your inner process. If you learn from your experiences and grow, your relationships will grow also.

A lot of these problems can be worked through by deeply and sincerely sharing your feelings, learning to take care of yourself, and by encouraging others to do the same. You may want to get support from a professional counselor or therapist to help you, or even your whole family, change old patterns.

*

I am
willing to reach out
for help.

*

Find supportive therapy

It has been my experience that many of us need help in the form of supportive therapy or counseling to deal with deep levels of emotional healing. For some of us, there is a certain reluctance to seek help, perhaps because we fear it is an indication of weakness, sickness, or craziness. Personally, I have sought therapy of various types at many times in my life and it has helped me greatly as long as I trusted my own intuition about who to work with, when to stop, and so on. We give ourselves a great gift when we ask for help.

*

*I have
the courage to ask
for help.*

*

Be honest

If someone in your life—a friend, lover, or child is being secretive or dishonest with you, ask yourself if you have been really honest about your own feelings, with yourself and with them. Is there some way in which you don't trust yourself, and therefore don't trust them? If we are afraid to be real and honest, we don't feel safe in the world and we don't trust others. Our friends and family may reflect this attitude. As we reveal and express ourselves truthfully, we will attract honesty and openness from the world around us.

*

*I am
honest with myself
and others.*

*

Children sense what you feel

If you are trying to appear calm and collected on the outside when actually you are feeling upset and angry, your children may mirror this to you by becoming wild and disruptive. While you are trying to maintain control, they pick up the chaotic energy inside of you and reflect it in their behavior. If you express directly what you are feeling, without trying to cover it up, they will usually calm down. They feel comfortable with the truth, the congruity between your feelings and your words. This is true of other relationships as well.

*

*When I
speak the truth, people
feel safe.*

*

Our relationships are channels

I move toward people I love because I want the intensification I experience with them. I feel the universe moving through me to them and moving through them to me. This may happen by just being together, talking, or touching. The intuitive energy itself lets me know what is appropriate. It's mutually satisfying and fulfilling because the universe is giving to each through the channel of the other. If I trust my own energy, each person in the interaction receives what they need.

*

The universe
is channeling through my
relationships.

*

Trust and appreciate your
sexual energy

We are beginning to be more open and natural about our bodies and sexual energy. Because of our old conditioning, however, many of us still believe on a deep level that our sexual energy is a sinful and dangerous force. We distrust ourselves.

In fact our sexual energy comes from the same universal source as all other energy. It is the expression of that energy that confuses us. We either exaggerate it or shut it off, fearing that we won't get what we need or that we'll lose what we already have. Sexual energy itself is innocent. It is merely one way in which universal energy moves through us and draws us to the experiences we need for our learning, healing, and enjoyment.

*

I *am*
willing to trust my
sexual energy.

*

Feel and enjoy sexual energy

To be in a state of innocence about our sexuality, we first have to recognize how we deny or distort our feelings. For example, if you feel attracted to someone you meet at a party, do you notice yourself trying to manipulate them toward a sexual encounter? Or, do you find yourself suppressing the sexual feelings because you're afraid, or you're with someone else? In both cases you've blocked the enjoyment of the sexual feeling you are having, either by racing ahead with it, or by trying to ignore it. *It is okay to simply feel and enjoy our sexual energy.* We do not need to make anything happen. If it is appropriate for something more to happen, it will happen in a relaxed, natural way. And whether or not anything happens physically, we can still enjoy the feelings and the energy.

*

*I enjoy
feeling my sexual
energy.*

*

Trust your rhythm

People sometimes push beyond their natural sexual rhythm, either looking to satisfy needs unrelated to sex or rebelling against suppressive sexual rules. This pushing can eventually diminish their sexual energy. They seek increasingly stimulating ways to satisfy themselves, but satisfaction eludes them.

You can trust that your energy will bring you what you need. You can trust that your own rhythm is unique and beautiful. You can relax, enjoy, and listen to your own rhythm.

*

*I respect
my own sexual
rhythm.*

*

Allow yourself to feel

Many people are frightened of their sexual energy and have protected themselves by cutting it off and denying it. This kills the sexual energy and leaves them feeling frustrated, afraid of themselves and their passions. As you begin to recognize the universal source of this sexual energy, you can accept the feeling, knowing you do not have to "do" anything about it. You can just begin to allow yourself to feel and enjoy it.

*

*It is safe
for me to feel sexual
energy.*

*

We are infinitely attractive

Many of us fear that we are not attractive or desirable enough to attract others. We have believed that we are "not enough." Today let's remind ourselves that we all receive our beauty, energy, and light from the same inexhaustible source. As we acknowledge this and begin to love and appreciate ourselves as we are, our channel opens and we have available to us the infinite vitality, beauty, and magnetism of the life force.

*

I am
attractive, desirable,
and lovable.

*

Receive appreciation

Imagine yourself in some everyday situation, and picture someone looking at you with great love and admiration, telling you something they really like about you. Now picture a few more people coming up and agreeing that you are a wonderful person. (Even if this embarrasses you, stick with it.) Imagine more and more people coming up. Picture yourself in a parade or on a stage and hear the applause ringing in your ears. Take a bow. Thank others for their support and appreciation.

*

*I am a
wonderful person. I deserve love
and appreciation.*

*

*Our bodies express our
individual perfection*

The body is continuously changing, replenishing,
and rebuilding itself at every moment, following the
guidance given to it by the mind. The more we bring
our consciousness into alignment with our highest
spiritual aspiration, the more our bodies will express our own individual perfection.

*

*My body
expresses my unique
perfection.*

*

Form a habit of being creative

Creative visualization is a basic and important tool in expanding our lives and creating our reality. Try creative visualization out in different situations and under different circumstances. If you find yourself worrying or puzzled about anything, or feeling weak, powerless, or frustrated about a situation, ask your intuitive guide whether there is a way you could use creative visualization to help you. Form a habit of being creative in every possible situation.

*

*Each situation
is an opportunity to be
creative.*

*

Visualize your perfect body

Get comfortable. Take a few deep breaths. Relax your body and your mind. Exhale tension, frustration, or tiredness. Inhale relaxation, strength, prosperity. Picture or imagine an image of your body. Imagine that you are now your perfect weight, size, shape, and strength. You are energized, strong, and powerful. When you imagine your face and body, sense your beauty. Look and feel exactly the way you want to. Feel what it is like to have a body that supports your spirit. You have beauty, strength, and energy.

*

I am beautiful,
strong, and
energetic.

*

Act as if it were true

By doing affirmations you are replacing the old negative voices with new positive ones. When you first start using an affirmation, you may not believe it. In fact if you already believed it, there would be no need to affirm it. It is important though, to try to tap into a *feeling* of belief and an experience that the affirmation *can* be true. Temporarily, at least for a few moments, suspend your doubts and hesitations and put your full mental and emotional energy into the affirmation. Act as if it were true.

*

I am
willing to believe
in myself.

*

Messages from our bodies

One of the basic principles of holistic health is that we cannot separate our physical body from our emotional, mental, and spiritual states of being. For instance, when we have a physical disorder, it is a message for us to look deeply into our emotional and intuitive feelings, our thoughts and attitudes, to discover how we need to take better care of ourselves emotionally, mentally, or spiritually, as well as physically. With this approach, we can restore the natural harmony and balance within our being.

*

I *am*
balanced and
healthy.

*

Our stepping stones to enlightenment

In this new age, many of us have a tendency to deny any negative feelings. We judge them as "bad" or "unenlightened" when, in fact, they are our stepping stones to enlightenment. Our so-called negative feelings or attitudes are really parts of ourselves that need recognition, love, and healing. Not only is it safe and healthy to acknowledge and accept all our feelings and beliefs, it is necessary, if we are to get in touch with the fears and pockets of blocked energy that are holding us back from what we want.

In this wonderful new age, "enlightenment" means accepting ourselves as we are. Anything we no longer need will naturally be healed and released.

*

*I accept myself
as I am, and release what I
no longer need.*

*

Becoming aware of negative beliefs

Our negative thoughts are valuable messages to us about our deeper fears and negative attitudes. These usually are so basic to our thinking and feeling that we don't realize they are beliefs at all. We assume that they are simply "the way life is." We may be consciously affirming and visualizing prosperity, but if our unconscious belief is that we don't deserve it, then we won't create it. Once we become aware of our core negative beliefs, they begin to heal.

*

As I *become*
aware of my negative beliefs,
I *heal them.*

*

Healing negative beliefs

Here is a powerful method to discover and begin healing your unconscious negative beliefs. Sit silently and get in touch with a particular problem. Using a pencil and paper, describe the problem. Ask yourself these questions: 1) What emotions am I feeling? 2) What physical sensations am I feeling? 3) What old tapes or old programming am I running in my head? 4) What is the worst thing that could happen in this situation? 5) What is the best thing that could happen? 6) What fear or negative belief is keeping me from creating what I want in this situation? 7) Create an affirmation to counteract and heal the negative belief. For example, if the old belief is "I don't deserve to have what I want," the affirmation could be "I deserve to be happy."

*

I release
old beliefs, and create new,
supportive ones.

*

We can reprogram our concepts

If we find that we are responding to our world in a way that is harmful or limiting, we can reprogram our old concepts and ideas about ourselves and about life. Because of the way the body and mind work together, and the constant mutual communication between them (the body registering information about the physical universe, transmitting it to the mind, the mind interpreting the meaning according to our experience and belief system, then sending appropriate messages back to the body), we are able to explore and release old beliefs that do not serve us. We can create, affirm, and visualize new beliefs that will serve us well.

*

My mind and
my body work together to serve
my highest good.

*

A powerful and useful message

We get sick because we believe on an unconscious level that illness is an appropriate or inevitable response to a situation or a circumstance. In some way, it seems to solve a problem for us, give us something we need, or is a desperate solution to an unresolved and unbearable inner conflict.

Rather than thinking of illness as disaster, we can think of it as a powerful and useful message. If we are suffering, it is a message that there is something to be looked at within our consciousness, something to be recognized, acknowledged, and healed. It may indicate that there is something about the way we are living that needs to be changed in order for us to be emotionally healthier.

*

I am now
listening to what my body
has to say.

*

We deserve healing

Disease is a message from our bodies telling us that in some way we are not following our true energy or supporting our feelings. It starts with relatively subtle feelings of tiredness and discomfort. If we don't pay attention to these cues and make the appropriate changes, our bodies will give us stronger signals, including aches and pains. If we still don't change, more serious illness can occur. Even if it takes a strong message for us to pay attention, there is still plenty of time to heal. We need only believe that we deserve it and truly desire it.

*

*I follow my
true energy and support
my feelings.*

*

Imagine yourself in perfect health

Sit or lie down. Breathe and relax deeply. Imagine golden healing light energy all around your body. Feel it, sense it, enjoy it. Know you deserve this healing. Welcome it. Send this special, loving, healing energy to any part of you that needs it. See and feel it being healed. Picture the problem gently dissolving and flowing away. Imagine yourself in perfect health. Think of yourself in different situations feeling active, radiant, and healthy. Pick affirmations that work best for you and use them.

*

*I am
now in perfect
health.*

*

**

Fall

**

Falling in love

Falling in love is the most thrilling and passionate experience in the world and of course we want to hold onto it. Because we recognize that another person has triggered this experience, we think it is he or she that is so wonderful. Actually, what we are experiencing is the love of the universe within ourselves.

*

I feel the love
and passion of the universe
within me.

*

You are seeing your own beauty

The next time that you feel a romantic or sexual attraction to someone, stop right then and acknowledge that it is your own beauty you are seeing. It is the universe that you are feeling. Keep reminding yourself that this is all part of your true love affair— with the universe, with life, with yourself.

*

*I am always in love—
with the universe, with life,
with myself.*

*

True passion brings us together

True passion brings us together, but fear often takes over shortly thereafter. The relationship may start to die almost as soon as it blooms. We panic and usually hold on even tighter. The initial experience of falling in love is so powerful, sometimes we spend years trying to recreate it. Often it's only when we give up and let go that the energy starts to flow again and we can touch that same feeling.

*

I

let go and

trust.

*

Visualize positive change

All too often in ongoing relationships we have gotten stuck in certain roles and images with each other which we find difficult to change. It's as if we've put ourselves and each other in certain boxes with certain labels on them. We find this very limiting and confining, but we don't know how to step out of it.

Begin to visualize and affirm new images for yourself and for the other person. See the potential for positive change within every person and every situation, and give energy and support to that positive change through creative visualization.

*

*I imagine positive
change in myself and in
my relationships.*

*

The potential for perfection

The potential for perfection lies in every relationship just as it lies within each individual. It's already there, we simply have to uncover it by dissolving all the layers of "stuff" we have put on top of it. Remember that perfection does not refer to some external model or standard, but rather the unique and changing perfection innate in every being and every connection between two beings.

*

I am
innately perfect and so is
everyone else.

*

Giving love to ourselves

When you are emotionally dependent on another person, life can become a constant state of fear. Because you depend on that person for your supply of love and protection you must control that source at any cost, either directly, by using force, or indirectly, using various manipulations. Generally this happens subtly. "I'll give you what you need, so you will be just as dependent on me as I am on you. That way you will keep giving me what I need."

We can stop this endless circle by feeling the love we can give ourselves. We can connect with the true and inexhaustible source of love within and feel the power of the universe protecting us and filling our needs.

*

I

*am whole and
complete.*

*

Seeing your own reflection

When a man is attracted to a woman, he can recognize her as a mirror of his feminine aspect. Through her reflection he can learn more about his own female side and move through whatever fears and barriers he may have to come to a deeper integration within himself. When a woman falls in love with a man, she is seeing her own male reflected in him. She can learn to strengthen and trust her masculine side.

*

I *see*
my own reflection
in others.

*

See desirable qualities in yourself

Get in a comfortable position. Close your eyes. Relax your body. Bring to mind one person whom you admire or are attracted to. Ask yourself what qualities you find most attractive in that person. Do you see those same qualities in yourself? If not, try imagining that you possess them. Imagine how you would look, talk, and act. Picture yourself in a variety of situations and interactions. Continue to do this visualization regularly while you are developing these desired qualities.

*

*The qualities
I admire in others, I have
in myself.*

*

Spiritual energy and sexual energy
are the same

Many people still suffer from the mistaken idea that spiritual energy and sexual energy are opposing forces, instead of recognizing that they are the same force. People sometimes deny their sexuality in order to be more spiritual, creating a tremendous conflict within themselves, and eventually blocking the very energy they are seeking. Actually, spiritual energy and sexual energy are simply ways of expressing love for ourselves and others. Both are very powerful.

*

I honor
my sexual energy as a
spiritual force.

*

The power to create and transform

Most of us have become masters at cutting off our sexual energy. We are afraid of ourselves and afraid of where our sexual energy will take us. We instinctively know that our sexual energy has the power to create and transform, and that there is nothing safe, stable, or sedentary about it. Our egos are afraid of this, so instead of trusting our natural instincts, we learn to suppress them. As we become more comfortable with our own inner power, however, we allow the natural expression of our sexuality.

*

My sexual energy
has the power to create
and transform.

*

Sexual healing

Write down all your negative beliefs, thoughts, and fears about sex. When you have done that, close your eyes and see yourself turning your fears or negative beliefs over to your higher power. Take a deep breath and relax. When this exercise feels complete, write correlative affirmations to help you counteract the negative beliefs that you have listed. Use these affirmations regularly. If you have deep fears or blocks that don't seem to be healing, let your intuition guide you in finding a good therapist or support group to help you. Imagine yourself and your life free from these old beliefs and flowing with loving energy.

*

*My life
is unlimited and flowing with
loving energy.*

*

Feel without acting

Pretend for a day, an hour, or however long you want, that you have no preconceived ideas about what your sexual feelings are and what you should and should not do about them. Let yourself feel them without needing to act on them.

Enjoy the experience of feeling like a sensuous, sexual being without needing to prove or accomplish anything. Keep the focus on your own body and enjoy feeling the life force within you.

*

I *feel*
the life force
within me.

*

A place of innocence

As we free ourselves from our rules, limitations, and rebellions, we are able to discover our own natural sexual flow. We can then move to a place of innocence with our sexuality. We can feel our energy as pure, as the force of the universe moving through us. We can begin to trust and experience our sexual energy without the influence of preconceived ideas. This will free us to be spontaneous.

*

I

am innocent and

spontaneous.

*

Our lives are filled with sensuality

Looking at a flower or having a moment of eye contact with someone can be as pleasing and fulfilling as a physical sexual encounter. Our lives are filled with the sensuality of the universe. Certain experiences may allow us to feel it more intensely than others. As we open to our own sensuality we experience more of the passion of life.

*

I *feel*
the sensuality of the universe
moment to moment.

*

Listening to ourselves

When we feel attracted to someone, we become afraid of their judgments or their expectations. We give our power away. Rather than trusting our intuition and expressing ourselves directly, we often put our trust in a set of rules about how we should behave. We become anxious, thinking "If I say this, he or she won't like it." Try saying exactly what you mean. Allow yourself to do what you want in the moment, not what you think others expect. Be honest with yourself. In this way we can learn to trust ourselves and to find true intimacy with others.

*

I
trust
myself.

*

Explore without expectation

Knowing that you will support your feelings in any given moment gives you the freedom and safety to explore your sexual energy without the expectation that it must be done "right." There are fears, excitement, and uncertainty surrounding sex as we start to explore our energy. All these feelings come to the surface to be healed. We can accept all of them without criticizing ourselves. The more we become able to accept these feelings, the gentler the process of exploration.

*

*All of
my feelings are
valid.*

*

Express your feelings

If you want to make love and your partner doesn't, or vice versa, support and express the feelings you have. Then try to really listen to your partner's feelings. If possible, see if both of you can go under the surface and look for the deeper feelings involved.

It may be that you and your partner need to talk about some unexpressed hurt or anger. Or one of you may need some time alone. Keep supporting and expressing what you feel, so the energy may move freely.

*

It is safe
for me to support and express
my sexual feelings.

*

A different form of sensuality

Be open to expressing a different form of sensuality than usual. This energy may lead you and your partner into simply sitting together, lying together, holding each other, massaging one another, dancing, or something else you don't ordinarily think of as sex, but which can be just as satisfying. Be true to your feelings and the right actions will emerge.

If you don't have a partner at this time, be creative in finding ways to express your sensuality individually or with a friend through dancing, massage, or whatever.

*

I express
my love and sensuality in
many ways.

*

Merging and separating

All beings have a deep yearning to merge with another being. When we feel mutual love and attraction with another person, we allow ourselves to merge energetically with them and experience that feeling of bliss. Then we need to separate again in order to re-establish our sense of our own individual identity. This is sometimes difficult, as we tend to hold on to that merged state, fearing that if we lose it we'll never find it again and we'll feel too alone. So we stay semi-merged and eventually feel resentful because we feel we have no personal space of our own. Sometimes we fight in order to create separation. We need to learn to separate cleanly and honestly by establishing our boundaries and taking the space we need. A good relationship is a constant dance of merging and separation.

*

I merge deeply
and blissfully; I separate
and take my own space
clearly and easily.

*

The keys to intimacy

A relationship becomes stagnant when people are no longer willing to tell each other how they really feel. When people first fall in love, they are eager to communicate their feelings because they are still getting to know each other and dependency has not yet set in. As soon as it does, people often stop sharing their true feelings, or they begin to manipulate, fearing they might lose the relationship. To keep a relationship as fresh and alive as it was in the beginning, keep sharing your feelings directly even though it may be a little frightening to do so. Vulnerability and honesty are the keys to intimacy.

*

I *share*
my feelings honestly with those
I *love*.

*

Be true to yourself

Passion disappears when we are no longer open to our feelings, when we sacrifice being true to ourselves in order to hold on to someone else. To experience passion, we must first be true to ourselves and then honest with others.

Passion in a partnership comes from true intimacy with each other. As we become an open channel for our feelings, we become an open channel for the passion and joy that can flow through us.

*

I *am*
true to myself and honest
with others.

*

The relationship will unfold

We must be willing to let our relationships reveal themselves to us. If we are true to ourselves, expressing ourselves fully and honestly, the relationship will unfold in its own unique and fascinating way. You never know exactly where it will lead. It keeps changing its mood, flavor, and form from minute to minute, day to day, and year to year. At times it may take you closer to each other, at times it may take you further apart, but each stage in the relationship is an amazing adventure when we are trusting the universe.

*

*My relationships
are unfolding in unique and
special ways.*

*

There is something to learn

People often wonder what to do when they are involved in a monogamous relationship and find themselves attracted to someone else. There is no simple answer to this question. Usually when we block the energy and deny the attraction, we find that it becomes a bigger problem. It's best to be honest with ourselves and our partner about the feelings. We need to look deeper within ourselves to see what it is that we are most attracted to in this other person. Perhaps it is a quality that is under-developed in ourselves and/or our primary relationship. The situation can strengthen our primary relationship if we are willing to learn from it and if we act with integrity. If necessary, get a facilitator to help.

*

*I'm willing
to learn and grow from every
experience.*

*

Everyone gets what they truly
want and need

A difficult situation in your primary intimate relationship can strengthen your ability to create a harmonious and more satisfying relationship, although it can be frightening because of its potential for emotional explosiveness. Stay open to the possibility that if you are completely honest, things will work out so that everyone gets what they truly want and need. You might find, for instance, that an attraction to someone else does not lead you into bed with them, but into another form of relationship which enriches all concerned.

*

When I'm
true to myself, everyone's
needs are met.

*

Keep telling the truth

When I am willing to be honest, ask for what I want, and share my feelings openly, I always find that the underlying truth in any situation is the same for all concerned. At first it may seem that I want one thing and the other person wants something else. If we both keep telling the truth as we feel it, sooner or later we will discover that we both can have what we truly want. We can trust that the universe wants us to be happy and fulfilled. We tell ourselves the truth; we tell each other the truth. This is love.

*

*The universe
wants me to be happy
and fulfilled.*

*

My commitment is to myself

For me, the primary commitment I make is to myself—to love, honor, obey, and cherish my own being. My commitment in a relationship is to truth and honesty. To anyone I love, I promise to do the best I can to tell the truth, to share my feelings, to take responsibility for myself, to honor the connection I feel with that person, and to maintain that connection no matter how the form may change.

*

I am
committed to
myself.

*

Allow the form to change

When we don't know how to allow the form of a relationship to change while still honoring the underlying love and connection, it causes pain in that relationship. When you are deeply involved with another being, that connection lasts forever. After you have learned a great deal from being with someone, the energy between you may eventually diminish to the point where you no longer need to interact on a personality level as much, or at all. Yet, the connection between your two spirits remains strong. Sometimes the energy renews itself again on another level.

*

*It is natural
and safe for my relationships
to change form.*

*

Communicating honestly can help

Changes in a relationship sometimes leave us feeling guilty, disappointed, and hurt. We don't know how to share our feelings effectively, so we respond by cutting off our connection with the other person. This causes real pain, because we are cutting off our own deep feelings. Changes can be relatively painless and even beautiful when we communicate honestly and trust ourselves in the process.

*

I *approach
change with honesty and trust
in myself.*

*

Every being is free to choose

For some people, being in a close, intense relationship with a person or persons of the same sex is the most powerful mirroring process they can find. I think many of these things are mysteries that we will understand only in retrospect, but I believe that every being chooses the lifepath and relationships that will help him or her to grow the fastest.

I do have a strong sense that on a spiritual level homosexual and bisexual relationships are a powerful step that some beings take to break through old rigid roles and stereotypes to find their own truth. The core purpose in every relationship is for each of us to find our own truth.

*

I accept
and honor each person's right
to choose.

*

Sexual energy is the life force

Sexual energy is passionate and vigorous. It is the life force (the creative force) of the universe. The key to a passionate life is to trust and follow the energy within us. The more we trust ourselves and move spontaneously with our energy, the more freely and fully the life force can move through us. We feel more deeply, and everything we do has an ecstatic, orgasmic feeling about it.

*

I *am*
a spontaneous, passionate
person.

*

Sexual energy meditation

Get in a comfortable position. Close your eyes. Take a few deep breaths and relax into that core place inside. Feel the energy of the universe pulsate from that core and move throughout your body. Know that this energy is sexual and passionate in its expression. See your sexual expression as the fiery energy of the universe moving through you to others. Imagine yourself expressing this passion to your lovers and your friends, in your work and creative projects. Know that the power within you is innocent, vibrant, and ecstatic. Know that you can trust the energy moving through you, that it is safe to express yourself.

*

*The power
within me is innocent, vibrant,
ecstatic.*

*

Physical exercise

No matter what type of physical exercise you do, you can use creative visualization and affirmation to help you get maximum benefit and enjoyment from it.

For example, if you like to run, picture yourself running very swiftly, smoothly, and tirelessly. If you dance or do yoga, put your awareness in your body, in your muscles; picture them relaxing and stretching; see yourself becoming more and more limber and flexible.

Use creative visualization to improve your abilities in your favorite sport; imagine yourself becoming more and more accomplished until you are truly excelling.

*

I *love exercising*
my body. I am strong, limber,
and physically fit.

*

*Limitations come from our
own resistance*

The only limitations on our health, beauty, energy, and vitality come from our own resistance to the goodness of life, based on fear and ignorance. There is, in fact, no evil or limitation. There is only ignorance or misunderstanding of the universal nature of good or God. We are in partnership with this all-powerful energy. The more we acknowledge and open to this power, the more good flows into our lives.

*

*I am
a limitless
being.*

*

Trust your body

Having a beautiful body starts with following the natural flow of your energy. We have been taught to distrust our bodies and see them as needing to be controlled. Trust yourself. Sleep as much as you want. Stay in bed if you need more rest. Express yourself physically in ways that feel good. Eat what your body desires and follow your heart. If you are willing to trust your body, you'll learn what's best for you.

*

I
*trust my
body.*

*

You are beautiful

When we are feeding our inner needs there is no reason to deprive ourselves of anything—if we want to lose weight, we will. The secret to having a beautiful body is simply to trust yourself and learn to follow your natural needs. Honor your intuition. Keep the energy moving by supporting yourself, moment by moment. Most importantly, love and nurture yourself. You are beautiful.

*

*I love
and nurture
myself.*

*

Eating ritual

Sit down with your food in front of you. Close your eyes, relax, and take a deep breath. Silently thank the universe for this food and thank all the beings who helped provide it, including the plants and animals, the people who grew it and prepared it for you.

Open your eyes and look at the food; really observe how it looks and smells. Slowly begin to eat, thoroughly enjoying the taste. Tell yourself that this food is being transformed into life energy for your use. Picture yourself becoming healthier and more beautiful as a result of eating this food.

Take a moment after you finish to enjoy the pleasant, warm glow that emanates from your stomach when it is satisfied and happy.

*

I

enjoy my
food.

*

Beliefs about our bodies

Most of us have negative beliefs about our bodies and/or the foods we eat. It is important to examine these beliefs and become more conscious of what we tell ourselves. Write down all your beliefs about food and/or your body. Write down anything that comes to you, even if it doesn't make sense or seem connected. Keep writing, the more the better. In making these beliefs more tangible, we are taking a most important step in our healing.

*

*It is safe
for me to look at my
negative beliefs.*

*

Origin of beliefs

Examine your present beliefs about your body. Try to remember where you first learned some of them. Did you pick them up from a parent, sibling, teacher, or a friend? Don't struggle to establish the origin of all your beliefs. Simply look at the ones that affect you most deeply, and observe the connections and memories that surface. Feel the feelings associated with these memories and consciously let them go.

It is an act of courage and self-love to look at the origins of your beliefs, to consciously feel and release them. The end result is a new sense of freedom and lightness.

*

I *feel*
lighter and
freer.

*

Identify the payoff

Look over your beliefs about your body and your looks and identify the ones that are not serving you now. Ask yourself what is keeping you from letting go of these beliefs. For example, a payoff for keeping the belief "I'll never be my perfect weight" might be safety. Perhaps it would be too frightening to receive the attention you might attract with a perfect body. It might be too uncomfortable to feel so powerful. Identify the payoffs you receive by holding on to your negative beliefs, and write them down. As you review them one by one, try to release these payoffs, and honestly feel how it would be to live your life without these fears.

*

I am
willing to tell myself
the truth.

*

Time to let go

When you have identified beliefs about your body that no longer serve you, it's time to let go of them. Realize they have served you for years. Thank them for the service they have provided and let them know you are willing to let go of them. Feel the release and freedom of being who you are now.

*

As I let go
of the old way, a new way
is shown to me.

*

Focus on what you like

Too often we focus on what needs to be changed about ourselves. We are waiting for perfection before we'll love ourselves completely. You can change this self-critical programming by looking at what you like about yourself and giving yourself positive feedback. Appreciate the beauty in your body and focus on the qualities you admire in yourself. Your body will respond to this appreciation and grow increasingly beautiful.

*

I *see*
many things I *like*
about myself.

*

Thank your body

Stand naked in front of a full length mirror. Focus on each part of your body. Find a way to appreciate every part of yourself and thank your body for being with you for all these years, following your desires and serving you. It has been doing what you have asked of it. If you like, you can play music that you love and use candles or flowers while performing this ritual. Do this once a day for at least a week.

*

My
*body is my
friend.*

*

A *physical expression of*
our consciousness

Our bodies are simply a physical expression of our consciousness. The ideas we have about ourselves determine our health and beauty, or the lack thereof. When we change our concepts on the deepest level, our physical self follows suit.

We are all in essence perfect spiritual beings. We are each a perfect expression of the universal mind or God-consciousness within us. As such, our natural birthright is radiant health, beauty, boundless energy, youthful vitality, and joy throughout our lives.

*

As I
*change internally, my body
changes.*

*

Beauty treatments

Do things for yourself regularly that make you feel you are taking special care of yourself and doing nice things for your body.

Take a hot bath or shower and visualize the hot water totally relaxing, soothing, and healing you. Picture any problems melting or being washed away, and nothing remaining but your natural radiance shining from within.

Put lotion on your face and body, giving yourself lots of loving attention, affirming that your skin is becoming smoother and more beautiful all the time.

*

I *regularly*
do nice things for
my body.

*

The universe is the true parent
of your children

In a sense, you don't have to raise your children at all. The universe is the true parent of your children. You are simply the channel. The more you are able to follow your energy and do what is best for you, the more the universe will come through you to everyone around you. As you thrive, your children thrive.

*

Each person
is a unique expression of
the universe.

*

Parents should continue to grow

For many parents, having children has been a convenient excuse for abandoning their own growth. They spend most of their time focusing on the children, making sure that they learn and grow properly. But in taking responsibility for the lives of their children, parents often abandon responsibility for their own, forgetting that children will respond positively when we choose to live our lives for our own greatest growth.

*

*I take
responsibility for my
own growth.*

*

Sense the powerful being within

This is the day for recognizing the true beauty, power, and magic within each other and in our- selves. Get comfortable. Close your eyes, relax and take a few deep breaths. Picture or imagine your child or your own inner child in front of you. Look into their eyes and sense the powerful being within them. Take enough time to receive feelings, ideas, or impressions about who your child really is. Com- municate to them your respect and appreciation. Imagine that your child is communicating respect and appreciation to you. Do this with each of your children or your inner child.

*

*I respect each child
and my own inner child as a
powerful, whole being.*

*

We all have healing power

A part of our consciousness is directly linked with everyone else's consciousness. Since this is also our link with divine omnipotence and omniscience, it means that we all have incredible healing power which we can tap into at will. If even one of us possesses the power to heal, in fact, we all possess the power to heal, and all of us receive that power from the same magnificent source.

*

I *have*
the power to
heal.

*

Healing meditation

Relax deeply. Think of yourself as a clear channel through which the healing energy of the universe is pouring. As clearly as you can, picture or think of someone who wants to be healed and ask him what he would like you to do for him in your meditation. See any problems in his body, mind, or heart dissolved, and see everything being healed and functioning perfectly. Surround him with golden healing light. See him radiant, healthy, and happy. Remind him that he is a perfect being. When you feel the meditation is complete, open your eyes.

*

*I am a clear
channel for the healing energy
of the universe.*

*

Trusting our natural flow

We are taught at an early age that expressing ourselves and fulfilling our needs naturally is not socially acceptable. Therefore, we learned how to suppress many of our natural desires, causing conflict and imbalance in our system and rebellion in our body and spirit. Often we react by going for the quickest available "high." Our bodies react to this imbalance by gaining weight, losing weight, becoming tense, or developing allergies and addictions. We crave all kinds of things we would not normally desire if left to our own natural flow.

We now have the tools to reconnect with our natural desires, honor the voice of our spirit, the voice of our intuition, which tells us what is best for us.

*

I *follow*
the flow of my natural
desires.

*

Become willing to receive help

Realize that we all use some form of addiction to pace ourselves, to keep ourselves from experiencing our own power and the power of the universe too fully. The cure for this is to build a trust in ourselves and the universe. Become increasingly willing to experience your own power and strength. For those who have a drug, food, or alcohol addiction, the physical craving overrides any awareness. The body and the drug are blocking any voice of the spirit. Help and support is needed. A professional substance abuse counselor or a group such as Alcoholics, Narcotics, or Overeaters Anonymous can help one abstain from drug or food abuse. This gives the body a chance to heal and the spirit a chance to be heard.

*

*I am
willing to receive help
from others.*

*

Addiction as control

The more uncomfortable we are about trusting our natural energy, the more likely we are to display addictive behavior such as excessive use of coffee, alcohol, unwholesome foods, drugs, overwork, and dependent relationships. Many people are afraid of being "too much" or "too little." Addiction becomes a means to pace, or suppress our power.

As we develop a trust in the universe, we are no longer overwhelmed by our own power and creativity. We are learning that surrender to this higher power is the path of healing. We can experience the ecstasy of being at one with the natural flow of the universe.

*

I trust
my natural
energy.

*

Assertion is vital

When we are afraid to be assertive, to express our true feelings, we may find ourselves using substances or people as a means of either voicing these feelings or suppressing them. The process of assertion is vital. As we back our feelings with action, we create an internal strength and protection. We feel safe moving into new situations, knowing that we will be able to say "no" to anything that doesn't feel good to us and "yes" to what does. We know that we will be true to ourselves and take good care of ourselves.

*

It is safe
for me to assert my true
feelings.

*

Make a contribution to the world

People often wonder what they are going to be when they grow up. What is it that they are going to do? What is their true purpose? Each of us has a true purpose and each one of us is a channel for the universe. When we follow our inner light, life is always fun, creative, and transformational. We make a contribution to the world just by being ourselves in every moment.

*

*I make
a contribution just by
being myself.*

*

Work and play are the same

Work and play can be the same. When you are following your energy and doing what you want to do all the time, the distinction between work and play dissolves. Work is no longer what you *have* to do, and play what you *want* to do. When you are doing what you love, you may work harder and produce more than ever before, because you are having fun.

*

When
I *work*, I
play.

*

The greatest reward

Let's make no more rigid categories in our lives—
this is work, this is play. Let it all blend into the
flow of following the guidance of the universe, and
money will flow in as a result of the open channel
that is created. You will no longer work in order to
make money or in order to sustain life. The delight
that comes from expressing yourself becomes the
greatest reward. The money comes as a natural
process of being an open channel willing and able
to receive the prosperity that is your natural birthright as a child of the light, as a divine part of the
dance of the universe.

*

As I express
myself, money flows through
my channel.

*

Working and receiving money

Working and receiving money may no longer be directly related to each other. You are doing what you want to do and money is coming into your life. It is no longer a matter of doing work and then getting paid for it. The two things may be operating simultaneously in your life, but not necessarily in a direct cause and effect relationship.

Trust that if you are doing what you love, the money will come. As you *give* love and joy to what you do, and as you *receive* love and joy from what you do, you are operating in a harmonious flow with spirit. The universe then becomes your employer, totally supporting you.

*

*I follow my
energy and the universe
takes care of me.*

*

Manifestation

There is no separation between us and God; we are divine expressions of the creative principle on this level of existence. There is nothing we have to try to achieve or attract; we contain the potential for everything within us.

Manifestation is the process of realizing and making visible on the physical plane our divine potential.

*

I am manifesting
my divine potential in every
aspect of my life.

*

Gratitude

On our path to the light, we often examine our growth with an eye to what we have yet to achieve. It is very important, however, to become aware of what we have already accomplished.

Make a gratitude list. Write down the ways in which you have changed, and the gifts you have allowed into your life. Acknowledge yourself for your dedication to spiritual growth. Consider how your family and friends have helped to bring you to this place on your path. Include those people who have served as great mirrors and teachers in your healing.

Close your eyes. Sense and visualize all the wondrous things that have happened, all the gifts you now have in your life, and give thanks for each of them with the whole of your heart.

*

I

am

grateful!

*

Attunement to your higher purpose

This is a good time to take a look at your past visualizations and notice how many of them have already manifested in your life. As you continue to express your gratitude for these, your ability to use creative visualization will expand and become a powerful force for creation. You will find that you become more and more attuned to and aware of your higher purpose.

Notice the elements that tend to recur in your dreams, goals, and fantasies and the particular qualities of the things you find yourself doing and creating. These are important clues to the underlying meaning and purpose of your life.

*

*I am
in touch with the purpose
of my life.*

*

Acknowledge our higher purpose

We all know in our hearts what our higher purpose is, but we do not often consciously acknowledge it. In fact, many of us seem to go to great lengths to hide it from ourselves and the world. We fear the power, responsibility, and light that comes with acknowledging and expressing our true purpose in life. Often we are afraid that our higher purpose means giving up everything that brings us comfort and love. In fact, our higher purpose and our greatest joy are always in perfect alignment.

*

I know
and express my higher
purpose.

*

We are in charge of our own journey

When someone dies, they are unconsciously choosing to leave this physical body. On the physical plane, it may appear that they are victims of disaster or deadly disease, but spiritually, they are in charge of their own journey. Their spirit knows what it is doing even if the body denies it. When you start to believe this, you will also feel it telepathically and it will ease the pain of your loss. It is possible to grieve while knowing that the higher self of your loved one has chosen this path at this time, just as you also will choose your path and your time.

*

I am
in charge of my own
journey.

*

Transforming the aging process

By living as channels for the universe, I believe that we can slow and transform the aging process as we know it. I think it is possible to become more vital, energetic, and beautiful as we get older, rather than less so. So let go of the old rules and the old limitations and begin to experience day to day the wonder of a limitless life, a limitless world, a limitless universe.

*

As I *grow older,*
I *grow more beautiful*
and alive.

*

Changing our deepest attitudes

Learning to use creative visualization can become a process of deep and meaningful growth. We often discover ways in which we have been holding ourselves back, using our fears and negative concepts to block ourselves from achieving satisfaction and fulfillment in life. The process of change that occurs does not occur on a superficial level, as through mere positive thinking. It involves exploring, discovering, and changing our deepest, most basic attitudes towards life.

*

I *am*
exploring, discovering,
and changing.

*

Face your fears

If you have a lot of heavy emotions riding on whether you attain a goal, you may tend to work against yourself. In that case, it may be most effective and appropriate to work first on your feelings about the matter. You may have to take a good look at what you fear about achieving or not achieving your goal. Affirmations and clearing processes can help you feel more confident and secure.

Once you acknowledge the emotions and fears you have about your desire, you come to a place of greater peace with yourself. Paradoxically, this often clears the way for the original goal to be realized.

*

I *am*
facing my
fears.

*

Be flexible

Going with the flow means keeping your destination clearly in mind and yet enjoying all the beautiful scenes you encounter along the way. If life starts taking you in another direction, be willing to change your destination. Be flexible. Savor all the surprises life brings, and life in turn will bring more and more wonderful surprises to you.

*

*I am
ready for life's
surprises.*

*

Everything is unfolding perfectly

You will find in using creative visualization that your ability to manifest will work to the degree that you are in alignment with your higher purpose. If you try to manifest something and it doesn't seem to work, it may not be appropriate to the underlying pattern and meaning of your life. Be patient and keep tuning into your inner guidance. In retrospect you will see that everything is unfolding perfectly.

*

*Everything
is unfolding
perfectly.*

*

Follow your intuitive feelings

Notice what happens when you doubt, suppress, or act contrary to your feelings. You will observe decreased energy, powerless or helpless feelings, and physical or emotional pain. Now notice what happens when you follow your intuitive feelings. Usually the result is increased energy and power and a sense of natural flow. When you're at one with yourself, the world feels peaceful, exciting, and magical.

*

*I am following
my intuition and my life
is fulfilling.*

*

Listen to the message

If you are feeling tired or ill, rest. Your body will always want rest and ease if it's sick. When you become quiet, ask your body what you need to do in order to heal yourself. Your body may tell you to: change certain habits, eat more wholesome food, express some feelings, quit your job, see a doctor, or it may have some other message for you, but there is always an answer available to you. The key is to ask and then listen honestly for a response.

*

I
listen to my
body.

*

Earth is our collective body

If you are concerned about environmental issues, consider this: Mother Nature is symbolic of the nurturing feminine aspect of ourselves. Disrespect and lack of harmony with nature are only possible in a society of individuals who disrespect and disregard their own feminine intuitive nature. If you are attuned to your inner guidance, there is no way you can become severely out of balance with your natural environment. In a sense, earth is our collective body. The way we treat her mirrors the way we treat our own bodies.

*

I am
in harmony with my body
and the earth.

*

Loving our earth

The lack of respect and attunement to our bodies is demonstrated on a global level by the way we treat the body of our planet. As we learn to trust and love our bodies, listen to their signals, give them food, rest, and nurturing, stop polluting them with drugs and unwholesome food, stop trying to control them with our artificial rules and ideas, I believe we will be able to treat our earth body with the same care and respect.

*

As I
nurture my body, I nurture
the earth.

*

Abundance is our natural state

There is more than enough to go around for every being on earth if we are willing to open our minds to the possibility. We are not yet experiencing our world as rich and abundant because we have not fully opened to the true nature of the universe. We believe in the inevitability of poverty and scarcity and do not yet realize that the ultimate power of creation rests in the hands, minds, and hearts of each of us.

*

I am
opening to the true abundance
of life.

*

A magnificent paradise

Picture yourself in a lovely, natural environment. Take time to imagine all the beautiful details. See yourself fully enjoying and appreciating it. Begin to wander and explore, finding more and more exquisitely beautiful environments of great variety. Use your imagination. See the world as a magnificent paradise in which everyone you meet is experiencing satisfaction and abundance. Enjoy it thoroughly. Go to other planets if you wish. There are infinite possibilities. Eventually come home happy and content. The universe is truly a place of incredible wonder and abundance.

*

The world
is my own magnificent
paradise.

*

As we change, our world changes

Because the world is truly our mirror, as we change, it must change. You can see this easily in your personal life. As you develop the habit of trusting and taking care of yourself, you will gradually release your old patterns. Soon you will notice that your friends, family, and business associates all seem to be reflecting this change as well.

*

Trust
and love begins
with me.

*

Change affects mass consciousness

Every individual's consciousness is a part of the mass consciousness. When a small but significant number of individuals have moved into a new level of awareness and truly changed their beliefs and their behavior, the change is felt in the entire mass consciousness. Every other individual is then moved in the direction of that change. The whole process may have started with one individual making the first leap.

*

As I
transform, the world is
transformed.

*

Transformation spreads rapidly

Transformation begins with an individual and moves out into the world. The more you trust your intuition and act on it, experience and accept your feelings, the more the energy of the universe can move through you. Everyone around you will benefit from your energy. It heals and transforms them. In turn, they become more powerful channels for everyone in their sphere of influence, thus transformation spreads rapidly throughout the world.

*

*My energy
heals and transforms
others.*

*

We see our reflection

Some believe that in order to change the world, all we have to do is think more positively about it and visualize the change we desire. Visualization and affirmation are powerful tools, to be sure, but there is more to it than that.

If the world is our mirror, then whatever we see out there in some way reflects what is in us. We need to take responsibility for it and be willing to transform it within ourselves if we want to see change out in the world. Looking at the world in this way erases all limited thinking and gives us the power to create a world of our choosing.

*

I take responsibility
for my outer world by taking
responsibility for my
inner world.

*

The world is my mirror

Notice the social, political, and environmental issues around you that trigger the most emotional reaction in you. Ask how they may reflect your personal issues, fears, beliefs, and patterns.

Ask for the light of the universe to release and heal all the darkness of ignorance, fear, and limitation within you and in the world. Regularly visualize your life and the world as you would like them to be. Ask your inner guidance to let you know clearly if there is any specific action you need to take toward your own or the world's healing. Then continue to trust and follow your intuition.

*

*The light
of the universe is healing me
and the world.*

*

Look for inner guidance

In the process of trying to create a better world, I find that people are frequently moved by their own "good ideas" more than by the universe within them. Often they are motivated by their feelings of pain, fear, and guilt into wanting to "do something to make the world better." This is the voice of the ego, coming from a position of helplessness and fear, struggling vainly to do something to eradicate these feelings. At these times we can check in with our inner self and see what action we are truly being guided to take.

*

*My actions
stem from my inner
guidance.*

*

Shine light in the darkness

When we are willing to recognize and heal any form of violence, poverty, and imbalance within ourselves as individuals, we begin to eradicate these problems from our world.

Healing does not take place on a personal or planetary level if we hide or deny our feelings. Our feelings, beliefs, and emotional patterns must be brought to the light of consciousness in order to be dissolved. When light shines in the darkness, the darkness disappears.

*

I accept
and embrace my darkness
and my light.

*

We are all co-creators

Do not take the blame or feel guilty for the world's problems. None of us is truly responsible for the lives of others. We are all co-creating this world together, and we are all doing it with limited knowledge. We are here to learn and we learn from what is imperfect rather than blaming ourselves for those imperfections.

We can adopt a positive attitude of responsibility by saying, "I am willing to learn to trust and follow my own inner truth, knowing that as I do, I will release the pain and fear within me, and thus help to heal the pain and fear in the world. I accept myself as I am."

*

*As I heal
myself, I help to heal
the world.*

*

Doing what you love

If you are trusting your intuition and following your heart, going where your energy takes you, and doing what you really want to do, you will see that your actions have a positive effect in changing the world. For many, this will include direct social and political action. People around you will be affected by your energy and vitality, even more than they are affected by your words and actions.

*

I am
now doing what
I love.

*

Transforming myself and my world

Get in a comfortable position. Relax your body and mind. Contact your source of strength. From this source, project yourself into the future a month, six months, or a few years. See yourself exactly the way you want to be. Start by noticing how you feel spiritually and emotionally. Because you trust your intuition, miracles unfold around you. See your body. You now have a body that matches your spirit, filled with life and energy. Notice how you dress. See yourself dressed exactly the way you want to be dressed. What is your home like? You have found a perfect job and creative outlet. You receive an abundance of money for doing what you most love. You now have relationships that are alive, passionate, and creative. Now, look out into the world, and picture the world as a mirror of the transformation that has taken place within you.

*

*The
planet reflects my own
transformation.*

*

The passion of life

When we trust and follow the energy of the universe within us, it leads us into the appropriate action for any given situation. It may lead us to speak or be silent, to move and dance or be still, to sing, shout, cry, or meditate. In interactions with others it may lead us to converse, to hug, to sit quietly together. The passion of life exists in all of these experiences and fulfillment comes from following and expressing this energy naturally, as we really feel it.

*

As I follow
and express my energy, I feel
passionately alive.

*

The spirit of giving

This morning take a few minutes to reflect on how you give of yourself to the world. Often we get caught up in the frenzy of buying and giving *things*.

Look at the ways you give appreciation, friendship, energy, time, love, and affection, and give of your own special talents and abilities throughout the year. Acknowledge yourself for having enriched the lives of others. Spend some time loving yourself for the giving light that you are.

*

I *honor*
myself for all that
I *give*.

*

Your own divinity

In the stillness of meditation be with your own divinity. Pause and quietly rejoice in the feeling of oneness with the universe. At some point in your life's path you became aware that there is more to life than what you perceive with your physical senses alone. At that moment your own spirituality was born in you.

*

I *celebrate*
the birth of my
spirituality.

*

What you create comes back

Whatever you try to create for another will always come back to you. That includes both loving, helpful, or healing actions and negative, destructive ones. This means, of course, that the more you use creative visualization to love and serve others as well as your own highest good, the more love, happiness, and success will find their way to you.

*

I *create*
the highest good for myself
and others.

*

The universe comes through many channels

When we feel an attraction to someone, it may be as brief as a glance or a short conversation with a stranger. It may be an on-going contact—a profound relationship that lasts for many years. Either way, we are experiencing the universe at work. In these encounters, we can see the universe coming to us constantly through many different channels.

*

I see
the universe in everyone
I encounter.

*

Trust the process of change

Real commitment makes no guarantees about a relationship's form. It allows for the fact that form is constantly changing, and that we can trust the process of change. It opens the door to true intimacy, created when people share deeply and honestly with one another. If two people stay together on this basis, they really want to be together. They continue to find an intensity of love and learning with each other as they change and grow.

*

*I am willing
to trust the process
of change.*

*

Your life is your work of art

I like to think of myself as an artist, and my life is my greatest work of art. Every moment is a moment of creation, and each moment of creation contains infinite possibilities. I can do things the way I've always done them, or I can look at all the different alternatives, and try something new and different and potentially more rewarding. Every moment presents a new opportunity and a new decision.

What a wonderful game we are all playing, and what a magnificent art form. . . .

*

*My life
is a work of
art.*

*

Visualize a more perfect world

It's fun and creative to take some time to visualize a more perfect, enlightened world. Use your imagination to transform things to your liking. Then write your vision in the form of affirmations. Acknowledge any fears that arise and create affirmations that will clear out those fears. Make a treasure map (a collage with pictures and words) of your ideal world. Look at your collage every day with energy and excitement. Let yourself fully desire that beautiful world and see it shining around you as you go through your day.

*

I *see*
a more perfect, enlightened
world.

*

A magical new city

I see an ancient city, gray and decaying. It is literally disintegrating, the old structures crumbling into piles of rubble. But it is being pushed aside, because in its place a beautiful, new city is arising. This new city is magical—it seems to shimmer delicately with every color of the universe. I know that it is being built inside of us. It is created from the light.

*

The light within me
is creating miracles in my life
here and now.

*

G L O S S A R Y

AFFIRMATION To "affirm" means to make firm. An affirmation is a strong, positive statement that something is *already so*. An important element in creative visualization, it is a way of "making firm" that which you are imaging.

CHANNEL "Being a channel" means being fully and freely yourself and knowing, consciously, that you are a vehicle for the highest creative energy of the universe.

CHANNELING Being in touch with and bringing through the wisdom and creativity of your own deepest source. (In this book, *channeling* does not refer to the psychic process of trance channeling, which involves a medium who goes into a trance state and allows another being to speak through him or her.)

FEMALE The inner intuitive energy of both men and women; the receptive aspect of our channel that allows the creative power to flow into us.

HIGHER POWER A higher intelligence, a fundamental creative power, or energy in the universe which is the source and substance of all that exists. Other terms often used to express this experience or knowingness, which is difficult to convey in words and rational concepts, are as follows: God, Spirit, Higher Self, The Light, The Universe, I Am, The Force, Source, Cosmic Intelligence, Inner Guidance, Christ Consciousness.

MALE The active energy of both men and women; the outflowing aspect of our channel that puts creative energy out into the world.

NEW WORLD Refers to a way of life based on an internal focus—trusting the higher power of the universe within and consciously allowing that creative power to move through us. In the *new world*, fulfillment comes from a growing spiritual awareness within.

OLD WORLD Refers to a way of life based on an external focus—without a fundamental spiritual connection, we attempt, in this *old world*, to find happiness and fulfillment through external "things"—money, material possessions, relationships, work, fame, good deeds, food, or drugs.

OLD FEMALE Refers to the traditional use of female energy (intuition, the door to higher intelligence) in which our male energy is used to deny and suppress feminine power, leaving us helpless, dependent, and emotionally unbalanced. (Both male and female energies are found in each sex.)

OLD MALE Refers to the traditional use of male energy (our ability to think and act) in which we suppress and control our feminine intuition rather than supporting and expressing it. Sometimes called "ego", its function is to hold onto individuality and separateness at any cost. Therefore, it denies the power of the feminine, which is a force moving toward union and oneness.

I N D E X

Abundance, 8/1, 8/16, 12/11, 12/12

Addictions, 11/20, 11/21

Affirmations, 3/10, 3/11, 3/12, 3/13, 3/21, 3/27, 9/22

Aging, 12/2

Anger, expressing, 5/14, 5/15, 5/16, 5/17, 5/18

Assertiveness, 5/17, 8/12, 8/13, 8/14, 8/15

Attraction, law of, 5/29, 5/30, 9/6, 10/7, 10/23

Being/doing/having, 1/21

Being here now, 1/15, 1/22

Body (healthy), 6/13, 6/14, 6/15, 7/17, 8/10, 8/12, 11/3

Body and self, 9/19, 9/21, 9/23, 9/27, 11/4, 11/6, 11/7, 11/8, 11/9, 11/10, 11/11, 11/12, 11/13

Caring for oneself, 4/13, 4/15, 4/16, 4/17, 7/21

Centeredness, 4/26

Change process, 8/9, 12/13, 12/14, 12/28

Channeling, 1/18, 2/8, 2/25, 2/26, 2/28, 4/27

Children/parents, 6/23, 6/24, 7/23, 7/24, 8/17, 9/11, 11/15, 11/16

Creative power, 1/5, 1/6, 1/17, 1/18, 1/29, 2/10, 3/31

Creative visualization, 1/8, 1/25, 1/26, 1/28, 1/29, 3/1, 3/2, 3/3, 3/6, 3/7, 3/8, 3/9, 3/14, 3/15, 3/19, 3/26, 3/30, 3/31, 4/24, 5/27, 9/20, 10/4, 11/1

Death, 6/12, 12/1

Decision-making, 7/5, 7/6, 7/7, 7/9

Dependency, 6/20, 6/29, 8/22, 9/7, 10/6

Divine potential, 1/27, 12/25

Earth, love for, 12/9, 12/10

Ecstasy, 4/12

Energy, blocked, 7/1, 7/2, 7/3, 8/11

Energy within, 1/9, 2/5, 2/15, 2/17, 2/29, 4/27

Enlightenment, 1/31, 9/24

Fantasies, 5/27, 6/2, 8/2, 8/3

Fears, 12/4

Feelings, experiencing, 2/12,
    2/13, 4/6, 4/8, 4/9, 4/11,
    5/12, 6/17
Female energy, 4/2, 4/4, 5/1,
    5/2, 5/3, 5/4, 5/6, 6/26,
    6/27, 7/11, 8/24, 8/26
Female/male balance, 7/10,
    7/12, 7/13, 8/19, 8/20, 8/21,
    8/27, 9/3, 10/8
Flexibility, 12/5
Forgiveness, 7/20, 7/25
Form, 1/24, 4/21, 4/22, 4/23,
    4/24, 4/25
Fulfillment, 1/20, 6/20
Genius, 2/9, 2/10
Getting what you want, 5/27,
    5/28, 5/29, 5/30
Giving/receiving, 6/7, 6/8, 6/9,
    6/10, 6/11, 12/24
Goals, 3/9, 3/16, 3/17, 3/18,
    3/21, 3/23, 3/25, 3/27, 3/28,
    3/30, 5/31, 6/30
Going with the flow, 3/29,
    12/5
Gratitude, 11/28
Grief, 5/20, 5/21
Groundedness, 4/26
Guidance, inner, 2/19, 2/20,
    2/21, 2/24, 4/29, 4/30, 5/1,
    7/5, 7/29, 8/21, 12/18

Harmony with universe, 1/23
Healing power, 11/17, 11/18,
    12/8, 12/19
Health, 4/14, 4/15, 4/16, 9/30
Higher power, 2/1, 2/2, 2/27,

Higher purpose, 1/19, 11/29,
    11/30
Higher self, 4/27, 4/28, 8/8
Homosexuality, 10/29
Honesty, 7/24, 9/10, 9/11,
    10/25, 10/26, 10/28
Hopelessness, 5/21

Illness, 9/28, 9/29, 12/8
Imagination, 3/6
Independence, 7/4
Inner guide. See Guidance,
    inner
Inner light, 1/7, 2/29
Inner sanctuary, 1/30
Innocence, 1/4, 4/1, 10/13
Intimacy, 7/30, 10/15, 10/20,
    12/28
Introspection, 1/3
Intuition, 1/10, 1/11, 1/12, 1/13,
    1/14, 2/3, 2/5, 2/6, 2/7,
    2/20, 2/21, 5/22, 6/16, 7/7,
    7/16, 8/8, 12/7

Learning process, 1/4, 8/4
Letting go, 1/16, 1/22
Life, choosing, 6/12, 7/7
Life force, 10/30
Limitations, 11/2
Living fully, 2/28
Love, 7/31, 9/5, 9/6, 10/1, 10/2
Loving oneself, 2/14, 2/22,
    3/28, 4/13, 4/18, 4/25, 5/12,
    8/30

Male, new, 7/13, 7/14, 9/2

Male energy, 4/3, 4/4, 5/1, 5/2, 5/3, 5/4, 5/5, 5/7, 6/26, 6/27, 8/23, 8/25
Male/female balance, 7/10, 7/12, 7/13, 7/15, 8/19, 8/20, 8/21, 8/27, 9/3
Mastery over life, 5/15
Meditation, 1/12, 1/15, 2/4, 2/19, 3/7, 3/9, 4/27, 10/31, 11/18
Mind/body, 9/27
Money, 4/5, 5/23, 5/24, 5/25, 5/26, 6/1, 6/4, 6/5, 6/6, 11/26

Natural rhythms, 4/4
Needs, expressing, 5/11, 5/13, 5/14, 5/17, 6/18, 6/19
Negative beliefs, 9/24, 9/25, 9/26

Old way, releasing, 1/2, 1/4, 1/6, 1/16, 3/13, 7/26, 7/27, 9/8, 9/22, 9/27, 12/19
Others, connection with, 2/25, 3/20, 3/26, 8/6, 8/7, 8/18
Outflow-inflow principle, 6/10

Passion, 10/3, 10/21, 12/23
Perseverance, 3/24
Power, 5/4, 5/8, 5/14
Problems in life, 7/28, 7/29

Relationships, 5/10, 5/11, 6/21, 6/22, 8/23, 8/24, 8/25,

8/26, 8/28, 8/29, 9/12, 10/19, 10/20, 10/21, 10/22, 10/23, 10/24, 10/25, 10/26, 10/27, 10/28, 12/28
Relaxation, 3/7, 8/11
Resistance to change, 3/13, 3/19, 4/9
Role models, 9/4

Sadness, 4/10, 5/18, 5/19
Self-acceptance, 7/19
Self-image, 4/20
Self-protection, 4/7
Sensuality, 10/14, 10/18
Sexual energy, 9/13, 9/14, 9/15, 9/16, 10/6, 10/9, 10/10, 10/16, 10/30, 10/31, 11/14
Sexual healing, 10/11, 10/17
Sexual rhythm, 9/15
Spirit, 1/24, 4/21, 4/22, 4/24, 12/25
Spirit of the Tao, 3/29
Spiritual energy, 10/9
Spontaneity, 7/22, 10/13
Surrendering, 2/17, 2/18

Talents, unique, 2/9, 2/11, 2/23, 2/24, 8/5
Therapy, 9/9, 11/20
Thoughts, 3/5
Transformations, 1/1, 1/8, 1/17, 4/24, 7/27, 12/15, 12/22
Treasure map, 6/30, 12/30
Trust, 7/18, 10/15, 11/19

Universe, energy, 1/5, 1/9, 1/10, 3/29, 4/4, 6/7, 6/8, 12/27

Universe as lover, 8/29, 8/31, 10/1, 10/2

Universe as parent, 11/14

Validating oneself, 5/8, 5/9, 5/10, 6/29

Vulnerability, 5/18, 5/19

Weight problems, 5/13, 8/12, 8/13, 8/15, 11/19

Wholeness, 8/19, 8/22, 9/7

Wisdom, 1/12

Work, 6/3, 11/24, 11/26, 11/27

World and change, 12/9, 12/13, 12/14, 12/16, 12/17, 12/18, 12/19, 12/21, 12/31

SHAKTI GAWAIN'S first three books (*Creative Visualization*, *The Creative Visualization Workbook*, and *Living in the Light* with Laurel King) have combined total sales of over a million and a half copies, with foreign editions in eight languages. Shakti lives in the San Francisco Bay Area and teaches workshops and seminars nationwide, as well as at her Shakti Center in Marin County, California and her retreat in Kauai, Hawaii.

"I give your books the credit for turning my life around. They give me the clearest guidance of anything I've read or heard. I can't thank you enough."

—MF, Arkansas

"Your work has been for us a kind of light illuminating all we have been seeking to realize. I would like to thank you for having so greatly benefited our lives and the lives of many others."

—UD, Brazil